The
Mystic Typewriter

The Mystic Typewriter

Rakesh Chopra

Published by
PRABHAT PAPERBACKS
An imprint of Prabhat Prakashan Pvt. Ltd.
4/19 Asaf Ali Road,
New Delhi-110002 (INDIA)
e-mail: prabhatbooks@gmail.com

ISBN 978-93-5521-386-0
THE MYSTIC TYPEWRITER
by Shri Rakesh Chopra

Edition
First, 2022

Price
₹ 250.00 (Rupees Two Hundred Fifty only)

Printed at
R-Tech Offset Printers, Delhi

And those who were seen dancing were thought to be insane by those who could not hear the music.

—Friedrich Nietzsche

Dedicated to
Neera, Rohan
& Sonu

Acknowledgment

No book can see the light of day without the help of many.

Foremost, I must thank Mr. Shiv Khera. His encouragement, help and initiative were invaluable.

I owe a great debt of gratitude to Mrs. Manjari Lopez. Without her tremendous input into proofreading and content improvement, this book would not be what it is. It was a labour of love to be engaged in this process with her. It was a reunion with a beloved teacher, and there was a constant feeling of déjà vu and nostalgia while we worked together.

I would also like to thank Mrs. Kiran Khera, Amrita Bhalla, Brig Kamal Nandwani and Rohan Chopra, for their guidance and suggestions.

Finally, I would like to thank Neera, my wife, as every book takes a big chunk of time, and without her sacrifice, support and understanding I would never have been able to complete such a venture.

1

He was unsure as to what had brought him to the tea plantation. Perhaps an aroma that lingered from a previous incarnation. He felt unknowingly safe, at home as though cocooned within a mother's womb, secure yet oblivious. The green colour all around him felt more like a river of emerald running through his being. The wide open spaces, the undulating countryside and the endless rolling hills, they invigorated him. The scattered tea-pickers with their woven cane baskets nestled on their backs and head-straps pressed tight against their foreheads, picking away in silence, dotted the landscape. They added a sense of ease. He felt one with every leaf, every grain of soil and in harmony with the hushed song of this foliage. This place was where he belonged.

The sun rose, seemingly in haste, dispersing the morning mist that sat upon the hills. It lingered, not wanting to let go, clutching at the tea leaves. It was a daily ritual between the two, nature's slow dance, centuries-old; on some days, it lasted for hours, others, minutes. They always parted. He slowly made his way back to where he lived. It was aptly called 'The Cottage'. It stood out amidst the surrounding expanse of tea gardens, imperious – quaint, picture-book-like, a landmark built by Indian hands for British whim in 1884. In bygone times it was the residence of the British tea-estate manager.

The narrow, much-trodden footpath of bronze coloured

mud roved about the bonsai tea shrubs and reached across the gentle hill to perish at the stone footsteps that led to the cottage.

It was nearing two years since he had stumbled upon this place. Why here of all places? That remained a mystery. It certainly did not seem to be of human design.

Demitri Kosatzakis now owned the cottage. One would never picture a Greek living out his days on a hilltop in southern India, but he had made it a deliberate choice. He had been a professor of Greek Scientific Mythology at the University of Athens who chose to retire to Munnar in southern India. The back-story was – he had visited this green pearl during his otherwise misspent youth and was smitten by a local maiden and mesmerised by the tea estates. He never managed to tie the knot with her, but a close second was to spend the rest of his days in the place where he lost his heart. His intense passion for tea was an accomplice to this decision.

Consequently, the day after he took his long-awaited retirement, he left Greece for India to spend the remainder of his life here. He was now nearing his seventieth birthday. Demitri had bought the cottage at a somewhat inflated price as the previous owner had wind that the foreigner's heart was set on it. Why he continued to live here, alone, away from his kind, never once travelling back to his motherland – well, that was a story for another day. He was now more native than the Keralites.

The cottage was indeed a prized property, standing aloof and elegant at the crest of a hill, overlooking endless acres of tea gardens as far as the eye could see. With its characteristic amber rooftop, it stood out amid this sea of green – it looked like a forelock on the head of a green parrot. It had become a local landmark.

Arvind ambled uphill towards the annexe of the cottage; he had let it from Demitri at a relatively nominal tariff. It was detached yet snug to the main bungalow and spacious enough to serve its purpose. It had a Victorian character to it.

There was a large bedroom with a high arched ceiling, with thick mahogany beams running across it. In one corner was an antique teakwood four-poster bed; an ageless, frazzled, rolled up mosquito net clung precariously around its edges. A side door led to a small, attached kitchenette. The cooking area looked out-of-date. In the corner was an old-fashioned wood-burning stove. The other side of the bedroom led to a spacious, comfortable living room, with a log fireplace in the centre of one wall and an ornate wrought-iron mantelpiece surrounding it. The annexe was conveniently secluded from view, so it was practically non-existent to anyone who had not visited the cottage. The anonymity served Arvind well.

He got along well with his Greek landlord, and they would often sit in the veranda of the main cottage at sunset and sip some homemade wine brewed by Demitri. Arvind felt that even the wine, somehow, was infused with the taste of tea leaves. Demitri would often delve into nostalgic ruminations once the grape elixir adequately saturated him. Occasionally he would ramble in Greek as if he were conversing with the Greek gods.

In the last two years, Arvind had almost become a native of Munnar. With time, any land and its inhabitants get used to each other. As though allowing for naturalization of sorts. It is a mutual acceptance. He knew the bylanes and many spots of untold natural beauty, unspoilt by tourists. There were long winding paths around the tea gardens that led to nowhere in particular. He sometimes wondered as to where they might have led to in historic times. He felt that these paths he walked upon now recognised and accepted his footfall. Was there a meaningful history buried in these hills? He could perceive it even though he did not know what it was. He wished he could have been a fly on the wall a few hundred years ago, long before the British landed.

It was just past seven in the morning. The world had not quite stirred to life. He knew that Demitri's maid would be another hour and forty minutes or so; he could enjoy the quiet, the stillness of the morning and the solitude before she started a babel of clanging pots and pans. Arvind stepped into the annexe through the unlocked door. He did not have much in worldly possessions; just plenty of old books that were of no value to anyone but him. A few photographs in a stylish but weathered shoebox were his only treasures. He never felt at risk of getting burgled.

He went straight through to the small kitchen and set a kettle to boil on the stove. The kettle was his favourite appliance and material possession, and he treasured it. He had acquired it from a retired school headmaster he had run into when he first got here. The headmaster mentioned something about it being an 'ancient family relic' that he wanted to get rid of as it was associated with sour memories. It was made from solid cast iron and was reassuringly heavy. Arvind always looked forward to his first cup of tea from freshly harvested Orange Pekoe tea leaves that he had acquired just the day before, once they had endured the seven stages of tea processing. It was a Saturday, so he had no plan for the rest of the day, except some reading, watching the news on TV – always with disgust – and gardening in his small allotment adjacent to the cottage. Of course, a few school children from the surrounding villages would come for 'science' tuition in the afternoon. Arvind did this because he could, and it was also a form of giving back to this community, which was now his new home. The living room would fill with children and their honest enthusiasm and earnestness for a short while. There would be no room for sorrow. At sunset, he would join his neighbour and let the wine ease the ache inside his heart.

He nestled down in his trusted rocking chair made of aged oak, and placed the pot of steaming brew in front of him. He was impatient to have his first sip as the steam from the kettle rose before his eyes, almost in sync with the mist coming off the hills. He cherished his first cup of morning tea, and this daily ritual. He always took his first sip in haste and let it burn the tip of his tongue as its heat set his throat ablaze. He felt alive.

As he rocked the chair rhythmically back and forth, his mind drifted back in time, perhaps still searching for an answer about why he had come to and stayed on, in this entirely unknown town.

He was not likely to get an answer yet again.

□

2

"Dr. Arvind ... Dr. Arvind," repeated my long-suffering secretary. She had put up with this madness for the last nine years at my busy medical practice in Bandra, Mumbai. I disliked the term, Bombay. For me, it would always be Mumbai – '*Amchi* Mumbai'.

My mind had drifted to just over three years ago. Dr. Arvind Bakshi, more popularly known as Dr. Arvind, or simply Dr. R. (Aar), I was a physician in this crazy, bustling but ever-amazing metropolis. I was forty-one years old, having trained at the best medical institutions in the country. Soon after completing my post-graduation and registrar training in Internal Medicine, I set up a clinic. I was amazed by how rapidly my success had come, perhaps because I had followed the 'ABC' of private medical practice – availability, behaviour and competence.

I was readily available to my patients, and they hailed as much from the ghettos as from the top-floor penthouses of the Mumbai skyscrapers. They could call me at any hour – and, by gosh, they did! Also, I was amicable, approachable and treated my patients like my extended family, giving them the full measure of my professional ability, care and concern. Sometimes, it was a heavy price to pay. From the first day at medical school, I was taught that a doctor must remain emotionally detached from patients. Somehow, I could never adhere to this universal mandate handed down to all medical students. My existence was intimately interwoven with them. It cost me countless sleepless nights, and my family too had to pay the price of this hedonistic dedication of mine. I had vowed to bc beside my patients through thick and thin, till the very end. To hold their hand firmly to their grave, if need be. Fortunately, I was reassuringly good at my job.

All of this, and the unknown overseer who shapes our destiny, made things fall in place. Unexpectedly and swiftly, I became one of the busiest and most popular practitioners in this suburb of the city. I had a roaring practice, and there was always a waiting list of patients pressing for an appointment. Hence, the reason why my secretary, Sangeeta, was greying rapidly.

"Dr. Arvind ... Dr. Arvind," she repeated with anguish in her voice. "Mr. Tuli wants an urgent appointment today, but you are already fully booked till nine p.m., and your wife is expecting you home promptly afterwards. What should I do?"

I knew Mr. Tuli well; he invariably demanded an urgent appointment – even if he had a small pimple on his cheek. "Fit him in early tomorrow; I shall see him before the main appointments start. That should appease him," I replied.

I took the 'Hippocratic oath' literally. It was written almost two thousand five hundred years ago by the great Greek physician Hippocrates. Every doctor has heard about it, but few know much about or care precious little for it. It is now more of historical curiosity. A dubious translation by James Loeb is as below:

'I swear by Apollo the Healer, by Asclepius, by Hygieia, by Panacea (as one possible explanation suggests: Apollo, the god of healing, fell in love with a human, Coronis. In his absence, Apollo sent a white crow to look after her.

When the crow informed Apollo that Coronis loved another man, Apollo's rage turned the crow black.

To avenge her brother, Apollo's sister shot Coronis with an arrow and, as she lay dying, Coronis told Apollo that she was bearing his child.

Although Apollo could not save Coronis, he rescued the unborn child, Asclepius. Hygieia, the goddess of health, and Panacea, the goddess of cures, are the daughters of Asclepius. According to legend, Hippocrates was a descendant of one of Asclepius' sons and by all the gods and goddesses, making them my witnesses that I will carry out, according to my ability and judgment, this oath and this indenture.

To hold my teacher in this art equal to my own parents; to make him partner in my livelihood; when he is in need of money to share mine with him; to consider his family as my own brothers, and to teach them this art, if they want to learn it, without fee or indenture; to impart precept, oral instruction, and all other instructions to my own sons, the sons of my teacher, and to indentured pupils who have taken the physician's oath, but to nobody else.

I will use treatment to help the sick according to my ability and judgment, but never with a view to injury and wrongdoing. Neither will I administer a poison to anybody when asked to do so, nor will I suggest such a course. Similarly, I will not give to a woman a pessary to cause abortion. But I will keep pure and holy both my life and my art. I will not use the knife, not even, verily, on sufferers from stone, but I will give place to such as are craftsmen therein.

Into whatsoever houses I enter, I will enter to help the sick, and I will abstain from all intentional wrong-doing and harm, especially from abusing the bodies of man or woman, bound or free. And whatsoever I shall see or hear in the course of my profession, as well as outside my profession in my intercourse with men, if it be what should not be published abroad, I will never divulge, holding such things to be holy secrets.

Now if I carry out this oath, and break it not, may I gain forever reputation among all men for my life and for my art; but if I transgress it and forswear myself, may the opposite befall me.'

Of course, certain aspects of this oath were obsolete and irrelevant to modern medical practice, but the core meaning struck a chord and deeply impacted me. 'I will keep pure and holy both my life and my art'. That was to be my professional compass. I aspired to be a physician 'par excellence', to uphold the highest ideals of the medical profession, for I believed that there is no greater honour bestowed upon man in the order of occupations than to have the privilege of being a physician. A profession where every encounter is sanctified, wherein the patient enters into a sacred bond. It means entrusting the physician with their body, in whatever measure, even for a brief period, decreeing the doctor as the guardian for their health and much more; submitting themselves to an intimate intrusion: physical, mental and emotional, and on even many other subliminal levels. Sadly, I had seen this privilege repeatedly and callously abused in the corridors of medical practice and vowed never to be part of it.

In the last few years in India, the practice of medicine had turned on its tail. The pathetic disdain for the inviolable profession of medicine by its guardians was abysmal and shocking to me. There were touts arranging hospital beds, agents selling kidneys for transplant surgery and local doctors referring patients for unnecessary investigations for kick-backs from labs.

Ghost surgeries, wherein a surgeon would perform the procedure, whereas the named surgeon would be different, were commonplace. Targets were set for each month and needed to be met for the number of procedures a surgeon must carry out for the hospital he was employed by, even if not indicated! Practitioners with roaring practices often treated their patients with casual dismissiveness. Whilst trivialising many ailments, they inflated or overstated others, leading to unnecessary and complex procedures and investigations. A doctor would often be seen conversing with one patient over the phone while pretending to attend to another. Long-buried was the sacred doctor-patient relationship; bedside manner was now just a namesake, with only a handful of physicians holding on to its fragile, sanctified threads. Unscrupulous malpractice was ubiquitous, all for the lure of money. I often wondered if Hippocrates was turning in his grave! I knew that I could not partake in such practices.

At the same time, I was also well aware that I had to get home on time today as I had promised my wife. We were to attend a dinner at my in-laws' home. Missing that would be an unpardonable offence in the unwritten bible of marriage.

My blessings did not end with professional success. I had married Anamika ten years ago, after a five-year courtship. She was the best thing that ever happened to me. She was kind and gentle – 'all soul', and managed beautifully to buffer and iron out any quirks and the many inadequacies that I had. She was a perfect template for all that I was not and did indeed 'complete' me. It was a much-blessed knot.

As I drove home in my shiny new Mercedes, an acquisition attributed to my financial success, I looked up and saw a photograph of our small family on the sunshade above, where I had tucked it in. I saw our eight-year-old daughter, Mehak, looking back at me with her smiling and beady eyes; she was a carbon copy of her mother, not just in her beautiful looks but also in her demeanour. That made me even happier. I whispered a small prayer of gratitude as I entered the underground parking for the apartment block in which we lived. Our home was on the eleventh floor. It was an elegant skyscraper on the posh Napean Sea Road.

My wife was happy and impressed to see me on time. She understood how hard I worked, and that it was necessary to stay on the treadmill of success in this over-commercialised world. We had a pleasant evening with my in-laws; we got along very well. I was always amazed that I had never had a cross word with my wife in ten years, given the nature of marriage. Life was carrying on blissfully, and I remained busy with work while my family stayed happy and contented. Mehak was an exceptionally intelligent girl; she excelled at her studies and had a strong inclination for the fine arts. She was already developing into an outstanding pianist and had performed three times at her school stage shows. Oh! What promise the future held for her. It set my heart ablaze with pride. Anamika also remained busy with her social services commitments. Being a Sociology major, she spent much of her time helping the ever-increasing autistic population of Mumbai and raising social awareness of this problem. I was surprised to learn how significantly the incidence of this disorder was increasing in the city.

It had not been an easy task convincing Anamika to marry me. I was a rather ordinary-looking man and had no 'tall, dark and handsome' attributes. I had a head full of thick black, curly hair and was about the body double for Sachin Tendulkar, which was, in fact, another handicap as she told me later.

I had first set eyes upon and met her at the steps of the Gandhi Memorial Library. At that time, I was a fourth-year medical student. I had come to the library as I needed to borrow some reference material for an article I was writing on the broad subject of 'Social ramifications of the dearth and sustained deprivation of core medical practice in rural India'. The main library building was undergoing some much-needed structural repair. Over the next few months, there was a makeshift registration desk outside the building, at the top of the footsteps to the library and access to the main library building was limited. She worked there as a part-time Assistant Librarian and was in charge of the membership and registrations on that particular morning. Along with many others, I, too, was in the queue, waiting for my turn to be issued with a temporary membership card to make use of the library.

Once I saw her, I just could not take my eyes off her. Although she was not a classic beauty, she looked pretty as a picture to me. Wearing a lilac coloured 'salwar kameez', she had tied her intensely dark mane of hair back into a tight bun; she had no make-up – I thought she did not need any. Her eyes had a gleam of innocence and kindness, half a smile seemed to linger at the corner of her mouth. She must have noted my repeated glances, so she was not smiling and was all business by the time I reached position number one. I, on the other hand, was fumbling and inarticulate and all thumbs!

Suppressing a slight tremor, I managed to hand over my driving licence as a photo identification document required to issue a library card. Having had my card issued, I made my way to the Sociology section. Little did I know that Anamika was doing her masters in Sociology and this section of the library was her particular domain as an Assistant Librarian. I was browsing through the Sociology section when she walked into the aisle a few minutes later. Seeing me there, she looked outright suspicious and all I got was a cursory glance. I continued my search to find the right book and finally found the one I thought was relevant. I walked up to the main desk to get it issued. She was sitting there, and again I could not help but notice how attractive she looked.

I cleared my throat and clumsily slid the large hard-bound, weather-beaten reference text forward on the desk towards her, and said in my best baritone voice.

"Could I please borrow this volume?"

She looked up at me, took a long pause and spoke, "I'm sorry, you cannot get this particular book issued. It's a 'reference only' text, and you can use it only within the library." I looked back at her a bit sheepishly, feeling like a dimwit and somewhat uneasy.

"Oh, hmm, I ... I see," was my rather feeble whispered response. I turned and made my way back to re-shelf the book.

"Excuse me," I heard a voice calling. As I turned around, Anamika gestured for me to return to the librarian's desk.

"Why do you need this particular volume?"

I explained that I was a medical student and needed it to research an article I was writing. It was then that she told me that she was a Sociology postgraduate student.

"I do own a personal copy of this book, and I could lend it to you," she said, sounding generous yet stern simultaneously. Rather an unexpected turnabout, I thought. However, I was the one in need.

"Oh! That would be helpful," I managed with a rasp. She

let me have her copy the next day.

That was how it all began. I promptly returned the borrowed book four days later, along with a small box of handmade chocolates. Nothing flashy; I did not want to make my feelings obvious. From then on, I was a regular visitor to the library on one pretext or the other. The main motive was to rest my eyes upon this exquisite maiden who had stolen my heart. My frequent visits and rather feigned studiousness mixed with sly glances did not go unnoticed by Anamika. However, there was no progress whatsoever on forging any sort of a relationship. My charade was to end soon. Once I finished writing my article titled, 'The long-term impact on rural health caused by the absence of a structured community medical care system', I decided to present her with a copy.

It was a daunting task. Not very apt at social skills related to the opposite sex, it gave me a couple of sleepless nights and required much preparation and rehearsal. Finally, on a Saturday morning, soon after the library opened and knowing that she would be there, (I had memorised the timetable of her shifts by now), I mustered the courage and, wearing a well-rehearsed smile, I walked up to her and presented her with a copy of the article.

"Since your help was invaluable, would you be interested in reading my finished article?" I asked with a faint tremor in my voice. She looked up, gave a coy smile and silently accepted. It had turned out to be a lot easier than I had anticipated!

I did not return to the library for another week. I was, somehow, apprehensive of her response, though I had no reason to be but for the nervous ruminations of an enchanted mind. Such are the perplexed travails of youth. When I returned, Anamika was not there; instead, the other Librarian handed me a square plain white envelope, without anything written outside. Inside was a card with a beautiful landscape – a print of 'The Cornfield' by John Constable on its front. Inside there was no printed inscription but a beautiful scrawl in purple felt-pen ink. It said how much she enjoyed the article, and she was impressed by the breadth and depth of the issues I had covered. It was signed 'Anamika Patel'.

Well, from that moment onwards, my joy knew no bounds! Baseless, the wanderings of my mind became expansive, limitless and even senseless. It lent me some confidence but still took me another three weeks before I could gather the courage to ask her out for a coffee. On this particular day, I waited outside the library approaching its closing hour, pacing up and down like an expectant father for over an hour, beads of sweat pouring on my brow. I almost jumped her as she came through the main entrance.

I even forgot to say hello and went straight to the point – "Oh! Ah! Umm...would you have coffee with me?" I blurted.

There was a pregnant silence. She was startled by my sudden appearance.

"Yes," she replied in a whisper after what felt like a lifetime.

I was unsure what to say next as I had not prepared for a response, much less a positive one. I had been so obsessed with just being able to ask her out on a date that I had even forgotten to pick a rendezvous. She half-smiled and walked away, and she was about ten yards away when I found my tongue and shouted after her.

"Ravi's Café, tomorrow, at six p.m."

She stopped, half-turned, and I caught a glimpse of a faint smile as she turned and walked away. The next twenty-four hours were spent in doubting and redoubting myself as to whether she had accepted the date.

The next day eventually dawned after what seemed like an eternity, and the night passed in oblivion. I dressed and got ready hours ahead of time, contemplating whether or not to take a bunch of flowers. It is impossible to read a woman's mind, and it was my first step into the unknown. I finally decided on a tame, clichéd book – 'Best-loved Poems'.

I donned my best shirt from my limited wardrobe and executed a surgically close shave and splashed on copious amounts of expensive, borrowed after-shave. I was at the café half an hour before the appointed time and chose the most discreet two-seater table, which also afforded a good view of the entrance.

Every minute seemed like an aeon, passing painfully slowly. My eyes remained glued to the windows and the main entrance. The entrance door jingled each time it opened; after a few times, it began to irritate me when I looked up like a desperate man, each time in vain, as it was always someone else. The appointed hour came and went, and the jingle was now a knell of disappointment. I had never wanted to see anybody so badly ever before. I tried to remain patient amid a million negative emotions. Hope still had its foot in the door. Around half-past 6, and by that time I was three cups of coffee down, I felt my pride folding. I waited another five minutes and just as I stood up to leave, the cafe's proprietor came up and handed me an envelope.

"A young lady came at five p.m. and asked me to give this to you at exactly thirty-five minutes past the hour. I was not to give it to you if you left before that. You fit her description," he recounted. It was from Anamika. I hastily tore open the envelope. Inside was a note stating. 'Seven p.m. at Saby's Chai Shop'. Saby's was another trendy youth hangout about a couple of kilometres away. There was just enough time for me to make it there. I somehow managed, given all the hitches of Mumbai traffic. I felt rushed, exasperated and flustered. By this time, my ego was starting to seethe at its fragile edges – my sanity held by the weak glue of a one-sided infatuation.

I entered the café and looked around, carefully scanning every nook and cranny. Anamika was nowhere in sight. I knew that I had been stood up. But as if that wasn't enough, I felt I had also been played. I was furious and hurt. I pretty much stormed out of Saby's.

"Hey, mister! Hey, mister!" Someone was calling from behind me as I was storming away from the cafe. I turned and saw the café owner; he rushed up to me and handed me a rose-coloured envelope. Enclosed was another note in a handwriting that was now familiar. "Tomorrow at six in Searock's lobby." Searock was a local and rather exclusive sea-front hotel in Bandra.

I was astounded at the audacity of this girl. If she thought I would go through all of this again, she was decidedly mistaken. There was no way I was going to subject myself to another humiliation. This affair was over before it had even started!

That night was a long and restless one. My soul was behest with conflict. After hours of tossing and turning in bed, my annoyance and disbelief reached a crescendo. I saw red. I tried to put on a logical hat, reason against my smouldering emotions, and make sense of it all. The pit of my stomach kept churning incessantly. It was a 'night of the knives', and there was this intense 'see-saw' within my being. My male chauvinistic and egoistical half was determined to see the end of it. On the other hand, my infatuated, desperate and hormone-laden self was in favour of ... one more chance. The conflict went on all night – I went to the 'fifth circle of hell' and back. By the break of dawn, I had convinced myself that I would attend the rendezvous. But, this would be the very last time. Maybe just to get some closure.

I arrived at the hotel lobby ten minutes late as I had to cling to the remnants of my tattered self-esteem. In a remote corner, already sitting there, looking pretty in pink attire and with a solemn half-smile, was Anamika. As I seated myself opposite her, she smiled bashfully. I remained expressionless and silent. As she looked up, I noted her eyes had a somewhat sad countenance.

"May I begin with an apology?" she started. "Please let me explain."

"About four years ago, when I was an undergraduate, I met this man. He was studying for a Ph.D in Astrophysics at the same university. He was attractive and brilliant. He initiated a friendship, charmed me and showered me with gifts and attention. He also quickly attempted to turn it into a physical relationship, so much so – he almost coerced me into one. Fortunately, I was able to get away, as some friends had made me aware of his chequered history, and that it was an established pattern of behaviour and he had 'used' many a girl who had succumbed to his charms. I was deeply wounded as I felt I was truly in love with him. I vowed at that point never to allow myself to fall easy prey to, or for that matter, trust any man – ever again! I wanted to see whether you would still come even though I had hurt your feelings.

"I wanted to see how you would react. It was an ego-check! To see whether it meant enough for you to come today despite what you felt after what I put you through. I'm sorry." She said this with an earnest, somewhat subdued tone and then lowered her gaze and fell silent.

I smiled on the inside but did not make my feelings obvious. A part of me was still hurting, as my ego was severely bruised, but at the same time, I was also melting like a snowman at the equator. My vision, however, was no longer clouded. Annoyance was turning into respect. My decision to come had been vindicated and I wanted her friendship more than ever.

I wish I could say it was all smooth sailing after that. Though a friendship began that day, and we started to meet regularly, there was a cultural chasm. I was a Punjabi lad with a liberal upbringing, and she was a hard-core Gujarati girl from a strict and conservative background. She was a ready friend, but romance? That was an entirely different matter. We had long engaging, meaningful conversations, some walks in the park, endless cups of coffee and ice creams and heaps of laughs. She was beautiful, gentle yet exciting, but there was no holding hands, no candlelit dinners or dancing cheek to cheek. It would be delusional to label this as dating. I wondered if there was a lingering suspicion of 'all men are the same' that still stood guard between us.

A year passed by in two shakes of a lamb's tail. Our friendship was well rooted, but there was no spark from Anamika's end. My one-sided 'love' was intensifying, yet my hopes began to falter. My dream of a romance was wilting for want of reciprocation. My rational half was starting to stutter. My heart, in contrast, held steadfastly. It wanted my love to touch the skies, to be free, to soar, mingle with the heavens, sing and dance amongst the clouds, or be a scintillating kaleidoscope of technicolour raptures! It craved rainbows and mandolins. I wanted to serenade, to proclaim it, to shout from mountain tops, but instead, all I felt was a sense of being in quicksand where either my ability to love or my sensibility would perish. There was this differential of love from my end and platonic friendship from hers. The dichotomy was relentless and punishing. How long could an impoverished romance last!

It is wondrous how much a heart can fool itself – prolong hope, and launch grandiose ships on a mere twig, a glimmer, a straw of an imaginary amorous relationship. The extent of self-deception a person in love will fabricate before they throw their hands up is infinite. How peculiar is it for a person to be living in a world of make-believe and fooling their adult mind into an infantile state? But there does come a time when even those blinded by love will find themselves at crossroads. So too, it was for me. Amid all this, I must add that she never gave me any indication that we had anything more than a special friendship. All the wantings were of my creation – illusory, desperate and unbridled.

In the meantime, on the professional front, I qualified as a doctor. But, amid this achievement and celebrations, there was a painful sense of incompleteness – my liaison with Anamika. For over a year and a half, I had to put up with the sniggers and caustic jibes of my friends. I had ignored their advice that our relationship was going nowhere. Now I stood firmly at the proverbial crossroads. It was decision time: my graduation ceremony would be decisive in more than one way – I pledged. To linger in an abyss of a going-nowhere relationship is soul-destroying, and the breaking point was nigh.

Nonetheless, I knew any decision was not going to be easy.

My intense fondness for her stood in the way. It was the eve of my graduation and I walked for hours in a fog of uncertainty and indecisiveness. I was deliberating, analysing, convincing myself, even fooling myself and conniving means of further self-deception and persuading myself to carry on regardless. The simmer, however, had come to a boil. It was now or never. I decided that I would make my feelings explicitly clear – that the candle of this relationship had consumed its wax, and either we take it to the next level, or it would perish as another tale of unrequited love.

When the moment came, and I looked into her eyes, I felt myself slipping into melting lava of helplessness once again. Somehow, a more profound strength prevailed this time around.

I looked unwaveringly at her and spoke in an exasperated tone, "This 'friendship' thing between us, it's killing me, and I cannot discern when the sun is setting, or the moon is rising. Life is getting blurred. I think it is about time." I took a deep breath. "I want to marry you, and I would like your answer by tomorrow. I will see you tomorrow afternoon at two, right here on the steps of this library where we first met, and if you cannot accept my proposal, then it shall be our last meeting."

I turned sharply and walked away.

"Arvind!" she called after me.

I stopped and turned. She walked up to me, knelt on one knee, raised her left hand to me. With a silver tear slowly tumbling down the right cheek and a smile to match, she spoke, "Arvind, will you please accept me as your companion... for now and evermore?"

I was stumped. It was double graduation.

□

3

He saw it shatter into a million pieces; the broken pieces of glass scattered everywhere, each tiny bit was heart-shaped with jagged edges that sparkled in a red magnificence. Curdled blood oozed from the edges. He had merely touched the heart with but a gentle hand, and it exploded! What happened? Arvind hauled himself out of another tiresome dream. Yet another one that he could not decipher.

Life will invariably break your heart – how badly, that is up to providence. How blunt an instrument that shall sear through your being? How intense will the storm be? That is all in the hand of Destiny. How she chooses to roll the dice; will you get a gentle number 6 or a humble 1? How often? How severely, for a short while or forever – is unfathomable by a human mind. His thoughts drifted uncontrollably to the years gone by, how things had come to pass, how a near-perfect existence had been demolished into nothingness by a solitary, decisive and unkind stroke of fate.

He remembered the lines by Orson Welles – 'Nobody gets justice. People only get good luck or bad luck.' A person cannot second guess their lot – you never know which sandstorm awaits beyond the quiet horizon, you cannot hide: and you may not run.

His thoughts returned to their blossoming friendship after that first meeting at the Searock Hotel. It was a one-sided romance riding on the back of a tortoise. How he had the patience to endure it, he didn't know! Oh, how things turned after graduation day! The world changed colour. Once you cross beyond the threshold of friendship, a new chapter unfolds quickly.

He and Anamika became even better friends and lovers – inseparable. To this day he was unsure what love is. Love, a mere four-lettered word. It's strange to define love in this modern world, with so many exotic and mystical definitions floating around. With endless poetic and luminous verses written. Does anyone know, or even remotely understand it? Can anyone define it? Are these the most misappropriated four letters in the English dictionary? Or are they painting the most sublime of human emotions? Perhaps, when your soul feels its highest bliss – it is as close as you are going to get to its meaning. He did not know!

He recalled their wedlock like it was re-enacting right before his eyes. They had wed on a beautiful spring day in the foothills of Mahabaleshwar in a secluded, modest resort. Both of them wanted to keep it small and straightforward. It was a wonderful day and after that, everything simply got better. She was an ideal wife and companion, and life felt like a bed of roses. It was a celestial marriage; indeed heaven on earth. He felt liberated, fulfilled and delved headfirst into his profession. His success soared. Money and fame were natural byproducts.

Anamika's pregnancy came as a beautiful surprise. But it was also going to prove a challenge – they were expecting identical twins. Thirteen weeks and four days into her pregnancy, she felt uneasy and had a feeling that something was amiss. To err on the right side of maternal instinct, they arranged an ultrasound scan. The news was devastating – one of the foetuses had stopped growing, and rather mysteriously, was not even visible any longer in her scan. The findings confounded Arvind's obstetric colleagues. They struggled to explain what the cause was. It was an unusual occurrence.

There is no blueprint or precedent on how to handle the

loss of a twin in the womb at this stage of pregnancy. To even guess what could or would have been. Or 'if only'. How do you grieve a possibility? Even though half of their dream was still thriving we were pushed, unsuspecting, fumbling into a dark cloud. No one had a clue as to what they could say to us, and we had to find some meaning somehow, some explanation – or surrender to the fact that there was none at all.

Well, the answer finally came when Mehak was born: her 'little feet' stepped into our lives, and she was one for the price of two. She took the presence of more than one child, being larger than life from the word 'go'. Maybe it was a promise she made in-utero to her lost sibling. Our spirits rose way beyond our expectations. She was our precious child.

She swept away, in an instant, with a brush of her permanent smile and beautiful eyes, her joyful laughter any 'what ifs' that remained. They evaporated from our consciousness. She slept all night without any trouble, rarely cried; just a delightful child, forever content. She always seemed to be at peace. Her first steps, her toddler years, were easy parenting. It's as though she had no DNA of distress in her at all. They never had any room for regret.

Alas! Like most things magical ... he drifted back to his present reality.

□

4

The first call came about ten minutes before closing time. I had just wrapped up my evening clinic, and the last patient had been a complex one. I was about to get up from my desk when the phone rang.

Sangeeta said on the internal line, "There is a call for you, and the person says it is an emergency."

"Sure, put them through," was my natural response.

There was a gruff male voice on the other end. "Mr. Arvind" resounded instead of the usual 'Dr. Arvind' or 'Doctor Sahib', so it was an unusual greeting.

He continued, "Mr. Arvind, how are you? Things going bery well, getting bery popular, are you? Eh! What are you going to do with all this money that you are earning – a fancy car, fancy flat?" he said in a thick Marathi accent.

"What the ... who is this?" I started.

The voice on the end of the line interrupted and continued, "As it is, you work so hard that you have no time to spend it. Why don't you share some of this easy money with others?"

"What?" I said in a raised voice, and the phone went dead from the other end.

'That was strange', I thought. I called out to Sangeeta, "Do you have any idea who that was?"

"No," she said. "He wouldn't give a name."

A prankster, perhaps, I thought, and carried on with what

I was doing, and soon I left for home. Driving down, I had an uneasy feeling about the call, but it vanished as soon as I saw the smiling face of my dear Mehak. Soon my busy life took over, and I thought no more of it.

A week later, at about the same time, a call came through; this time, it was on my mobile phone. It was the same voice.

"Mr. Arvind, how are you? You should think about changing your car!"

The line went dead even before I had a chance to react.

This time I sat down and thought this was more than a prank call. As it was past the closing hour and I had stayed back by myself to look through some reports, I decided to lock up and head home. I turned out the lights of the clinic, enabled the clinic alarm. I walked hurriedly towards my parked car. With utter disbelief, I saw that there were multiple deep scratches on the paintwork, up and down both sides of my car, gouged out by a sharp tool, such as a screwdriver. It looked terrible. Scarred. Mutilated. Not one to be scared easily, it sent a chill down my spine.

It was then I realised that the phone call was not an empty threat. I immediately called the police, a faint tremor in my fingertips as I punched in the numbers. The local police knew me well, and they often came as patients. I had been accommodating and generous to them with my time and care over the years. They were with me within ten minutes. They did not seem surprised to see the state of my vehicle; obviously, it was something they had encountered before. When I mentioned the two phone calls, the sub-inspector looked up at me grimly and spoke, "Doctor, I'm afraid we may have a problem on our hands."

"What do you mean?" I asked, perhaps, intentionally being naïve as I did not want to believe it was anything serious.

He said, "We have recently seen a spate of activity where shop-owners, doctors, and other successful small businesses are targeted. The idea is extortion. The perpetrators usually start with telephone calls and intimidating messages, and small acts of vandalism follow. If they don't get what they want, they escalate their threats, and it turns into more serious criminal activity. In some cases, kidnapping and even murder are committed. Unfortunately, the Mumbai underworld is involved, and they often have political insurance. The dirty trail runs all the way to the top. No one to this date has been caught, incriminated or indicted. Such activity is conveniently blamed upon the international mafia. The phone calls often come from Dubai through untraceable SIM cards. The money trail also seems to be running all the way there."

"Surely there must be something we can do?" I asked.

"We can try, Doctor; we will register a formal FIR (First Information Report) complaint by you straightaway. I will run a trace on your mobile phone. It is, however, likely to be a blind alley," he said hesitantly.

I thanked the police and got into my car, and drove in a maze of disconcertion and upset. They had perturbed me and ruffled my feathers, very much as they intended. I decided not to tell Anamika, as I knew it would give her much angst. I tried to be strong and pragmatic.

The next day I called the Commissioner of Police and our local Member of Parliament. Both were my patients. They pledged their full support and promised to look into the matter expeditiously. A police constable was posted outside the clinic from the very next day. I thought the Member of Parliament, Mr Pramod Sinha, would be a strong ally in this battle. He was a close family friend and often came over to our flat. Anamika had worked with him on social issues in his constituency. He always praised her to the rafters, though, I must admit I disapproved of the way he looked at her.

The calls fell silent for the next three weeks. The car looked as good as new with the paintwork restored. The police had tried to trace the number from which I had received the call; as suspected, it turned out to be a blind alley. It was a Dubai-based SIM that the caller had used; there was no further information available. The Commissioner of Police seemed sympathetic. He made some hollow promises but it was soon evident that he was impotent. The police constable at the clinic was a mere token of deterrence. Our politician friend was silver-tongued and emphatic that he would get to the bottom of it straightaway. Somehow, I was not convinced. I started to hope against hope that it was something that may somehow disappear into the woodwork, and I may never get any more calls. However, as it turned out, it was merely wishful thinking!

A third call came after the clinic had closed for the day; it was just as I got into my car. It was as though somebody was watching me.

"Mister Arvind."

It was the same voice again. It was getting uncomfortably recognisable, but this time around it was harsh, and sounded more like a forced whisper and laced with intimidation.

"Mister Arvind, you are a strange man. The police, the Commissioner and your pathetic politician friend – they cannot protect you. We will not go away, and the only person who can make us go away is you. Fulfil our demands, and we shall leave you alone. Or else! Better check the brakes of your nice little car when you drive home to your wife and daughter tonight. Your daughter, she has pretty eyes, and your wife, she has lovely long hair," he hung up. I stared at the phone for a long time as I sat in the car.

It felt surreal. I was stunned and deeply perturbed – 'was this for real, or am I in some sadistic Hollywood time-warp movie?' Sadly, the reality check did not take long. I was unsure how to respond or what to do next – other local politicians were unlikely to be of any use. The issue was either above their heads or, more likely, they were involved.

Of one thing, I was adamant. I was not going to give in to their unveiled threats.

□

5

The next two months were harrowing. There were further phone calls and many small acts of vandalism. The aggravation was unrelenting, sometimes in the form of broken clinic windows; at others, cow-dung smeared at the clinic doorstep. These events were interspersed with more frequent telephonic threats by the extortion gang. The hardest part was keeping these occurrences from Anamika and Mehak. I wanted to shield my family from this ordeal. So far, there was no severe vandalism and none directed at them. I also struggled to maintain my focus at work, and I could be irritable at times. I was undoubtedly losing sleep, and when I did manage to get some, it was restless, with haunting and strange dreams. This matter was slowly beginning to take its toll on my health.

Then one day, it happened. I got a call from Anamika while I was in the middle of my morning clinic – not something that occurred very often. She sounded upset. She said that there was a dead parrot in our letterbox. She was not sure that it was just a prank from a teenager in the neighbourhood, as someone had also rung the doorbell but vanished by the time she opened the door. She was a bit disturbed, so she called.

I reassured her falsely, thinking to myself that this was getting too close for comfort. They had turned the heat on. It was an overt threat. I was now rethinking my stance of never giving in to their demands. They were asking for a lot of money, but what price is too much to protect one's family? It would burn a giant hole in my pocket, and an even bigger one through my heart, having to give out my hard-earned money to such unscrupulous and ruthless criminals. It was against my idealistic principles. But the paradigm had shifted.

I decided to try one last avenue. I recalled I had an old and dear friend in RAW (Research and Analysis Wing). We did not keep in touch much these days but used to be close friends during our school days, and had followed each other's careers. RAW headquarters is housed in a humongous brick-faced building in New Delhi. It is our foreign intelligence agency. It is brimming with resourceful and dedicated people. It was my last ray of hope before giving in to their demands. I called the agency and left a message for him.

That same evening, I received a callback.

"Hello Arvind, how are you? It's Krishan, and I just got your message. What's up? Good to hear from you, a pleasant surprise! It's been many years. I hope all is well at your end."

I hesitated, took a deep breath and said, "I'm afraid not." my voice laden with worry and apprehension. I quickly apprised Krishan. He remained silent for a while and then spoke, "Give me a couple of days; there is more than one gang embroiled in this racket, and the trail usually leads to the mafia. RAW does not normally engage in these issues; most of our time is invested in anti-terrorism activities and matters of national security. Of course, I have some connections. I would suggest that why don't you quietly and discreetly send your family out of town for a few days, as these guys can be dangerous, and retributions are ruthless and often involve close family. These people are evil."

I mumbled a raspy, "Thanks."

I tactfully arranged for Anamika and Mehek to go to my in-laws' house in Pune, three hours away; under the pretext that her parents needed help with re-decorating their home. I had set it up covertly and in confidence with my father-in-law.

I waved them goodbye in the very early hours on a Saturday morning under cover of darkness, with more than a heavy heart. I followed the car with a helpless gaze as it disappeared around the bend. I looked up at the sky and saw an umbrella of very dark clouds moving in.

It looked like there was a big storm brewing.

□

6

"Dear Mehak," he wrote painstakingly at a slow pace with an ailing ballpoint pen. The ink stuttered, flowing hesitantly, on the last page of a tattered notebook that was lying around. It was in the early hours of the morning, perhaps three or four hours past midnight. At that hour, the plantation is as quiet as it can be. Even the tea leaves are in slumber. It was the excessive alcohol inside him that gave him the strength.

"Dear Mehak, there is so much I want to say to you. Eight years were just not enough; they passed in a heartbeat, and I don't even know where they went. I never even got enough chance to tell you how beautiful you are. To be able to comb your long hair or braid it into pretty, long plaits. To buy you some more pretty dresses, and to listen to you play the piano. To hold you so tight that it hurt. If only I could, just one more time. If only you knew how my weary heart pines for you ... for your smile. You were my sunshine...I love you so!"

He felt like '*Deirdre of the Sorrows*'.

He hoped that he could shift the burden his heart bore on to the paper. It would not relieve the pain but may afford some balm and numbness to his soul. The pen slipped out of his hands, dropped onto the floor and rolled under the desk. Arvind slumped on the desk in a drunken stupor.

The following night, however, there was a set of formal letter-writing paper and envelopes and a new set of pens on his desk, and not a drop of alcohol in his veins. He decided that he would write a proper letter every night to his beloved daughter. He had gone into town and bought some stationery earlier that day. He wanted to turn a new leaf, to shed his gloom and depression. He was determined to help himself and let go of his past, no matter how tragic it was. Expressing his feelings on paper might help, in spite of how painful it may be. He hoped against hope that some stellar force would mystically send the letters forth to her to a nether land, to wherever she may be, in whatever metaphysical state, even if she were a spirit or a ghost. He remembered hearing a story about Oscar Wilde, who was a great man of letters, and as he was busy being brilliant, he would write a letter, paste a stamp and throw the envelope out of his window. He trusted that someone would pick it up on the busy London street in front of his house and post it for him, and it would find its addressee. Arvind was hoping for some supernatural magic. If nothing else, the letters would serve as a means for some emotional catharsis – a form of therapy for his broken heart.

It was that night for the first time he heard a faint sound 'Chik-chik-cha-chik-chik-chika-chik-cha-chikchick'. He had finished his second letter to his departed child and fallen asleep at the desk; it was again well past the midnight hour. The sound aroused him from his listless sleep. Initially, Arvind thought it was an apparition – an auditory hallucination. It lingered for a short while and then stopped. He fell asleep, and the sound came back again a few minutes later. He perked up, listening intently; he was sure it was familiar, and he had heard it before somewhere. He strained to place the sound, but he simply could not. 'Where could it be coming from?' thought Arvind. There was no one around for miles, just tea leaves rustling in a gentle breeze. The good old Greek next door was undoubtedly in a deep stuporous sleep, given the amount of home-brew he drank every night. He could not be generating any noises except for his porcine-like snore, which Arvind was accustomed to by now. 'It must be my imagination', he decided. He got up and went to bed. He felt a strange, uneasy sensation for most of the following day.

The next night he sat down to write another letter. Once again, in the still of the night, he heard the same sound 'Chik-chik'; it had a treble and a thump, a clunk and a timbre like no other sound. He was getting more confident that he had heard the sound before; he was at the brink of a deja vu moment, just that he could not recall where. The harder he tried, the less he could remember. The next evening, as he was preparing a cup of tea, and as his trusted kettle was just about starting to make a pre-boil rumble, it suddenly came to him! It was the unmistakable sound of a typewriter. An old typewriter ... An old Remington typewriter ... an ancient Remington typewriter ... a 1950's Remington!

"That's it!" he exclaimed loudly to no one but himself in his empty annexe – it was a rare flicker of excitement from him.

"I knew ... know that sound!" It had transported him right back to his early childhood.

His late paternal uncle had owned one such Remington. It was a rather well-used machine, and he used it daily, primarily to write letters of complaint. He would write to any and everyone who ticked him off or caused him any grievance, headache or heartache, or sometimes for no reason at all. It was 'Mission: Letter-writing' with him. The typewriter was his trusted weapon. He wrote to government agencies, councils, electricity boards, temples and social organisations and the water-supply people, lawmakers, the police and even charities. He was always admonishing them, chastising them, advising them, and criticising them for their blatant incompetence, how they had let this country's people down and how the motherland is being poorly administered at their callous hands. How corrupt he felt the system was and how his country had been sold down the river time and again. No one took him seriously. His letters went unanswered more often than not. An occasional agency would write to him, some respectfully apologetic and others telling him to mind his own business. He could remember his eccentric uncle typing away, day after day, sitting at his worn-out, chipped and wobbly walnut desk – one of its legs was short and supported by folded paper at the bottom. 'Chick-a-chik ... ' all whilst Arvind, a small child then, played with his worn-out abacus in one corner of his uncle's small living room. Arvind had heard hours of this sound for days on end. It was a sound from his childhood, etched into his auditory memory. It was a part of him. He was surprised that it took him so long to recall it.

From where could this sound be coming? The only other human within about two kilometres' radius, and that too an inimitable one, amid millions of tea leaves was Demitri. Even so, he did not own a typewriter as far as Arvind knew. Nor had he shown any inclination towards any letter-writing or literary pursuit. He made a firm note to solve the mystery the following morning.

The next day drew in quickly, and soon after breakfast, Arvind knocked on his neighbour's door. "Demitri, good morn, my dear man! Have you been hearing any strange noises over the last couple of nights?"

As expected, "What noises?" was the response from his half-awake neighbour. He was still rubbing his red, sleepy eyes, and he smelt like a damp brewery. He scratched his hairy, fat belly where it spilt over the waistband of his striped pyjamas. Arvind wished he hadn't rushed it and allowed the man to get over his hangover.

"I slept like a babe in arms," continued Demitri.

"I'm sure you did. But can you concentrate for just a couple of seconds and think if you heard any noises?"

"No, sir – Zilch!"

"Well, I did. So will you keep your ears alert if you hear anything?" requested Arvind.

"Sure, my good friend," said the Greek in an alcohol-tainted baritone voice.

"You wouldn't own a typewriter by any chance, would you?"

"Ha, you are jokeeng weeth me, Arvind?" his strong Mediterranean accent was evident.

"I hate those damn machines; they gave me arthritis." He started showing his knobbly fingers. With that, they returned to their homes.

That night Arvind did not write as he felt shattered. He stayed awake for most of the night, ears transfixed, waiting, but he could not hear any mechanical sound. He also began to question his sanity. Were these mere sounds rising from his tormented soul? A couple of nights later, he sat down again to pen a letter to his child. And sure as the full moon that shone down on the tea estate, the sound returned. He was awake and lucid. Now he knew for sure that it was not his imagination. Arvind's first response was to reassure himself, 'I haven't lost my mind.'

He virtually jumped up, quickly threw a nightgown over his shoulders and stepped out of the annexe; the sound seemed to be coming from Demitri's cottage. He snooped around its perimeter. All the lights were out, and there was an audible soft snore filtering through the windows of Demetri's bedroom. The 'chick-a-chik' could still be heard, but he could not localise from where the sound was emanating. Within a couple of minutes, the sound died down. Arvind had to return to his house.

The mystery had deepened. He thought he might as well wait and see.

The following day while Arvind was cooking an omelette, there was a knock on the door. His concerned neighbour and friend was at the door, and he looked pensive.

"Arvind, I was thinking, my cottage does have an attic, and that has some stuff in it. The previous owner told me so, and he promised to have it all removed within a few weeks of my moving in, but sadly, as fate would have it, his heart gave up on him and he left for his heavenly abode before that could happen. In all these years, no one from his family has come asking for it. Would you like to have a browse around to see if the noises are coming from there? Perhaps there is an animal."

"That sounds like a great idea, Demitri," although he was sure it was not any creature who was the culprit.

"See you a bit later then." He turned and left.

Arvind went about his daily chores. He would pause now and again to consider what could be in that attic that could produce a sporadic, spontaneous noise of an old typewriter; that too in the middle of the night. Was he getting delusional? He once again had a pang of self-doubt.

They ascended through the square trap-door on the ceiling of Demitri's bedroom with the help of the built-in loft ladder, the attic turned out to be deceptively large. It reminded him of the 'Tardis' from the 'Dr Who' television series, considering how huge the space had turned out. It was musty, dusty and smelt of a bygone age, but more amazingly, it was filled with dozens of artefacts. There were lamps, paintings, furniture, antiques, floor-standing fans, carved solid-oak desks, numerous wooden chests with locks on them, curios of various sorts, stacks of piled-up old books, stuffed animals, and dozens of cardboard boxes sealed with duct tape – some marked and some unmarked. It was like stumbling on to an ancient, forgotten warehouse. Some of the stuff had dust-laden drapes over them, others lay bare. There was a maze of dense cobwebs everywhere, made by laborious spiders over many years. It was messy trying to get past their clinging.

Amazingly, Demitri had never bothered to venture into the attic, and he felt little attraction for material possessions. He did not want to be lumbered with additional inconveniences.

The tea estate, tea-drinking and wine were where his world lay. He was satisfied by looking out across this vast expanse of glorious green landscape, day after day. Also, how was he ever supposed to know that it contained this much stuff?

Arvind flicked on his torch and Demitri followed closely behind, coughing and spluttering with dust billowing from the floor with every step they took. They found an empty light socket and put in the spare bulb which they had sensibly brought with them – the illumination transformed the attic. Things were much clearer now. The attic now looked more like a museum. They spent a couple of hours moving things around to make enough room to move through this treasure trove. Demitri repeatedly cursed under his breath for being the one who came up with the idea in the first place.

So far, there was no sign of a typewriter. Arvind thought there seemed to be a desk whose edge was just visible behind a tall cupboard in the room's far corner. He then decided to remove the thick tarpaulin covering it; as it came off, gusts of dense dust dispersed everywhere. Demitri had a severe coughing fit; then he started wheezing and almost choked. Arvind was genuinely astonished by what he saw: an old Remington typewriter was sitting right in the centre of the desktop, proud and glistening. Even though he had identified the sound, he never half-expected to find one! He stepped closer and touched it: a tingle ran down his spine. What was even more astonishing was that it was completely free of any dust, as though it were in a hermetically sealed glass cabinet and not in a dust-soaked attic, which had virtually invaded and permeated every other object there. It was clean and shiny as could be, as though it were in a factory shop window.

He shouted out to the Greek, "Hey! Demitri!" Who came closer and inspected the discovery and almost shrieked.

"Oh, thee-mou!" he screamed in Greek, which translates to 'Oh! My God!' Then after regaining his composure and his rational brain, he whispered. "Ah! The dust somehow has not gotten een to it."

There were two loft windows to the attic, firmly locked, and no doorways to access the attic other than from Demitri's bedroom. The haunting question now was: 'Is it possible that the sound that Arvind was hearing was coming from this typewriter? If so, how was it physically possible? What were the odds of someone using this typewriter?'

As Demitri would put it ineloquently, using his favourite word:

Zilch!!

□

7

Arvind instantly and severely missed his family from the very moment that their car was out of sight. It wasn't the first instance they had taken the trip to Pune without him but he felt a void, and oddly uneasy. Perhaps, it was to do with all that was going on and he was scared and worried. Fortunately, his wife and daughter were unaware of the circumstances of duress under which he had to send them away. That day he went to work with a shroud over his usual, cheerful countenance. His shoulders slumped and his head was downcast. He felt anxious, yet he repeatedly tried to pick himself up but kept slipping back into a state of despondency. His patients too noticed that their doctor was not himself. His aspect that day was quite uncharacteristic of him. They generously returned some of the compassion he always showed them. The day dragged on at tortoise pace, and Arvind could not shrug off his low temperament.

As the evening set in, Arvind was desperate to get home; it was unusual that he had not had a call from his wife confirming their safe arrival in Pune. He had been so busy that he had not had much chance to think about that. She often stopped at Khandala while travelling on this route and took Mehak for a picnic, which often delayed them getting to Pune. When the phone rang, he assumed that it was Anamika. Instead, it was a male voice, which sounded solemn: the caller was a sub-inspector from the police station at Lonavala.

"Am I speaking to Dr. Arvind Bakshi?"

"Yes," I replied.

"My name is sub-inspector Prabhakar, I am sorry, but I have some extremely distressing news," he continued.

"There has been an accident about three kilometres short of Khandala. A car ended up in the ravine below. It happened in the early hours of this morning but we have been able to retrieve the car only a short while ago, and when we traced the number plate, we found that you are the registered owner." He then read out the number plate – and sure enough, it was the car that Anamika and Mehak were travelling in.

"How are my wife and daughter?" I said with a squeaky outcry.

There was a pause and a short silence that felt like an eternity.

"I am sorry, Doctor, none of the three passengers has survived. We cannot even identify the bodies due to the severity of the burns."

The phone slipped from Arvind's fingers, and he slumped to the floor in disbelief; this was not happening! It was simply impossible, and the call must be a hoax, a cruel prank, he said to himself.

"Hello ... Hello! Hello!!" the voice at the other end was still online.

Arvind very slowly retrieved the dangling phone. The sub-inspector very gently and politely asked if Arvind could come over to identify the bodies.

The news had just mercilessly jerked the carpet from under Arvind's feet. He lapsed into a state of shock, followed quickly by frenzy. He ran out of the clinic, leaving his patients and staff confounded. He jumped into his car and took off for Khandala in a reckless haze. He risked his neck repeatedly, exceeding the speed limit by far for the most part. He wove in between cars, trucks, and other vehicles, narrowly missing them several times. He seemed to be unaware of his behaviour.

Once on the highway, he was speeding consistently over 160 km an hour; he seemed oblivious of his speed.

As Arvind was approaching Khandala, he saw two police cars parked by the roadside; an ambulance had already passed him, going the other way about twenty minutes earlier. Arvind slammed his car brakes, jumped out of the car, leaving the driver-side door open, and rushed towards the police cars.

"I am SI Prabhakar," said a benign-looking officer, guessing it must be Arvind. "I have been trying to call you to tell you that the bodies are on their way back to Mumbai in an ambulance, but I got no response on your mobile phone." Arvind realised that he had left his phone back at the clinic.

Prabhakar continued with genuine empathy in his voice, "I am truly sorry about what has happened, doctor."

"What exactly happened?" I asked, breathless and still trying to get hold of my senses.

"We are not entirely sure. It occurred early in the morning, and the traffic is sparse at that hour, so we have no witnesses. It was reported to the police control tower when smoke was seen rising from the ravine below. A passing army three-ton truck noticed it, and it was the driver who alerted the police. The emergency services have been working non-stop, but getting the mangled wreck up has been difficult. We managed to do so just before I called you. I am sorry, sir.

"I'm afraid a post mortem will be necessary, given the nature of the incident. It is a mandatory legal requirement."

"I will make my way back to Mumbai. Which hospital are they headed for?" I asked and ran back to my car. I was soon on the highway and speeding again. This time I was ambulance-chasing.

I wanted to arrive at the hospital at the same time as the ambulance.

□

8

Demitri Kosatzakis was born in Cyprus in the East Mediterranean, to Greek parents, who returned to Greece when he was three-years old. His father was a fisherman, uneducated but sharp as a knife. His mother, a petite and affectionate woman, was a folk dancer. He had no siblings. He was supposed to be christened Dimitri but the clerk at the birth registry office misspelt it as Demitri and the name stuck.

From a very young age, Demitri showed exceptional academic promise. He was speaking with a sound vocabulary by the age of two. His father was insistent that he must not go into fishing and make something of his life and take their future generations towards a different profession. School was a breeze for Demitri. He was always at the top of his class without much effort, aided by his photographic memory and high intelligence, only ever needed to read something once.

A restless teenager, he was quite partial to the opposite sex as he was growing up and as a young man had many affairs which never lasted as he was not interested in any long-term relationship. He had a finicky, cynical and unsteady disposition.

He was deeply interested in the quirky, ancient and bygone eras. By the time he decided to become a historian, he had already got a masters in Maths. He had a deep interest in the origins of his own culture, history and mythology of his country and the world, so it was no surprise when he steered his career in that direction, obtained a quick Ph.D, and to no one's surprise, Dr. K. was given a professorship at Athens, becoming one of the youngest professors at the university. A historian who was also good with numbers, a rare breed!

He did extensive research, published many papers on his chosen subject and became internationally renowned as an authority. His personal life, however, was a bit topsy-turvy primarily due to his growing love of alcohol. The addiction got so severe that he had to go into rehab. Once he was out, dry and clean, while still on sick leave and recuperating, he decided to have a holiday outside of Greece. He specifically wanted to go to India, primarily due to its great history, mythology and culture which resonated with his own country's.

He decided to start with Kerala – 'God's own country'. He spent a few days in Kochi and the backwaters of Kerala and then travelled up to Munnar, which tourists often do. He checked in at a quaint hotel in the middle of a tea estate originally built by Germans, who still owned part of it. The estate was now managed and run by a local family; it was here that he first saw and met Meenakshi. It was love at first sight, not surprising as she was an exceptional dusky beauty. So taken was he that he stayed for six months instead of his planned three weeks: his enchantment by the surrounding tea estates was a close second.

His affection was duly but secretly returned. He had never felt this way about any girl or woman he had met. They communicated in their broken English and a language of the heart that did not need many words. He proposed quickly, and that is when the trouble began. Meenakshi was a conservative Brahmin girl and when their affair came to light, there began a chain of catastrophic events – the girl was badly beaten by her parents and sent away to live with relatives in another town.

He tried to find her but could not. Distraught and desperate, he did not know where to go or what to do. One day he received a letter from her which said she did love him, but her mother had vowed to end her life if Meenakshi did not end the relationship. She begged him to return to Greece and never come back. She said that this would be his testament to their true love and his parting gift to her. That same evening, he returned to Athens, broken-hearted. He did not return till forty years later. Now he planned to stay till his last breath.

Now here he was stood, early in the morning, at his friend's door again, with nothing of his past haunting him: he had made peace with it a long time ago. It was uncharacteristically early for him as he was normally lost to the world till about ten a.m.

"Hey! Arvind, I have been thinking, and it might be a bizarre and irrational thought; still, I wondered if we should feed some paper into that typewriter to see if it prints something and whether the typing sound is truly coming from that machine. Of course, I don't expect it to have any ink, but then again, looking at its almost new condition, anything is possible."

"That would be something." Arvind quipped although he did not believe that it would be a fruitful exercise. But what was there to lose!

The following day they both clambered back up into the attic. Arvind went up to the Remington, fed an A4 sheet into the paper table and turned the platen knob ever so slowly. Surprisingly, he noted that the ribbon, the ribbon spool, and the ribbon vibrator seemed to be in mint condition and working smoothly. For someone devoid of a single squeamish bone in his body, he felt an eerie sensation run through his entire body and got goosebumps.

For the next three nights, he did not write a single word and stayed awake most of the night, dozing off intermittently, waiting and anxious to hear something. Not a single sound came from the attic or anywhere; just the tea leaves fluttering in the wind. The typewriter was quiet as a mouse, and the paper remained blank.

On the fourth night, he sat back at his desk to write again. He wondered why he never thought of writing to his wife. She had been his rock, his dream girl, and it was a privilege to have been married to her. Just thinking about her was enough to dismantle the fortress of resilience that he had built around his aching heart. That was not the reason though; somehow, the voice from within only called out to Mehak. Inexplicable, but that's just the way it was. Sometimes, a child can be more than the sum of its parents!

As he finished penning down another letter and exhausted, in an emotional cloud, about to crawl into bed, it was precisely then that the 'chik..a..chik' started again. Arvind wanted to run and climb into the attic, but knew that his inebriated friend would not appreciate a midnight call.

By the time dawn broke, Arvind was desperate and wanted to break down his neighbour's front door and clamber up to check the typewriter. He had to wait for what seemed like an age outside the Greek's bungalow. As soon as he heard some rustling in Demitri's house, he rushed to the door and knocked furiously. Demitri responded after many minutes and slowly opened his front door. Arvind did not wait for any pleasantries; he brushed past Demitri's flabby wine belly, rushed into the bedroom and scrambled up into the attic via the loft ladder. His reluctant, sedentary neighbour followed grudgingly, rubbing his sleep-laden eyes, grumbling in Greek.

The typewriter stood silent and still, expressionless almost mockingly. Arvind crept up close to it and stared at the paper they had fed into the typewriter.

His pupils dilated with utter disbelief! Was this an apparition, an illusion? He almost held his breath.

There was print on it!

"No!!" exclaimed Arvind.

"What happened?" mumbled Demitri, breathless, as he tried to catch up with him. Once he reached Arvind's side, he saw what had excited his friend.

"I don't believe thees. Thees is a joke, no?"

They both reached out and extracted the sheet of paper ever so gingerly rotating the platen knob. There, in front of them, was verbatim the letter that Arvind had penned to

Mehak the night before! 'This phenomenon cannot be possible,' thought Arvind. 'There has to be some logical explanation or some trick.' His knees trembled in sheer amazement.

"Demitri, this is word for word what I wrote to Mehak last night!"

"Not possible," responded Demitri.

"How can it be?" exclaimed both in unison!

They examined the sheet of paper again, closely and carefully; sure enough, it was true. The typeface was the typical old-fashioned monospace serif font of a Remington!

They descended from the attic in a daze and sat in Demitri's living room for a while in baffled silence. They were both men of science. The supernatural was an absurdity and unacceptable to both. They could not fathom what was going on. It was incredulous, yet it was factual.

Finally, the Greek broke the silence. "What do we do now?"

Arvind shook his head in utter disbelief, unable to respond.

"Let's see if this happens again. I am going to get a locksmith to check the loft windows and also get a lock on the loft trapdoor," suggested Demitri.

Arvind shrugged shoulders, still lost for words. Why would his neighbour want a locksmith? It was pointless. He realised it was because Demitri was scared!

"You continue writing your letters, Arvind. Let's see what materialises," he repeated.

They parted company in a state of bewilderment. The following day, by the time Arvind met up with his neighbour, the locksmith had been and gone from the cottage, bemused why the foreigner wanted locks fitted in these odd places. He couldn't remember the last time there was a theft in these parts. Anyhow, he was happy for the easy money.

That night Arvind was at his desk again. An hour or so after he finished writing the letter, the typewriter sound kicked off. This time both men were ready and waiting – they rushed up to the attic. Once again, there was a typeset on the paper.

But, there was no activity. Of course, there was nobody there, not a sound, just a machine staring back at them. They were spooked! They stared blankly at the typewriter and searched every nook and cranny of the room. There was nothing to find; Demitri made sure all the newly fitted and bolted window locks were secure. They returned and stared at the typewriter sitting majestically on the desk top.

The enigmatic only became more absurd. There was no rational explanation. This chain of events went on for three days in a row. These occurrences were getting bothersome and disturbing. On the third day, there was nothing new except some wood shavings lying around the bottom of the desk on which the typewriter sat.

"These were not there a couple of nights before. What was their source? Is there also a bloody rat in my attic?" exclaimed Demitri. The two men racked their brains.

Then Arvind said, "We need to find out from where these wood shavings are coming." Demitri got a bright torchlight, and while he shined the light, Arvind got down on all fours and crawled all around the desk. He found a small area at the back of the desk where he saw something etched into the wood panel just above the fallen wood shavings. It read:

V 103.

He read it out to Demitri; they swapped places so that his friend could see for himself.

"V 103?" repeated the Greek.

It meant nothing to them. They could not be sure that the shavings were fresh, although it seemed so. Was it of some relevance? There was no way of knowing. The engraved marks looked freshly made. For the next few days, the typewriter fell silent, making the two gentlemen question their sanity once again. Demitri confessed he was getting a bit scared and having restless sleep with nightmares.

Then one night, it started again! Sure, as day, Arvind's letter was in print – verbatim! Some more wood shavings and this time on the other side of the heavy mahogany desk was the same etching, 'V 103': These were undoubtedly fresh. What could it mean? Was it something or nothing? Just a bizarre co-incidence? Or was someone or something trying to send a message? Was there a ghost lurking in the attic? Somebody had to be doing the typing and the etching!

Since Arvind carried so much emotional baggage, he wondered, despite the physical evidence, whether his traumatised mind could be playing tricks on him! He knew that he most certainly suffered from post-traumatic stress disorder. It was almost inevitable after such a sudden and shocking loss. People can get visions, and imaginary sensory phenomena can happen. But then what of his learned friend, who had seen it all play out before his eyes? Was there some unusual history associated with the cottage? Maybe it had something to do with black magic! Something perhaps, only the natives would understand or decipher; after all, they were both immigrants to this land. Arvind was only two years old here and Demitri a dozen more. Was the attic haunted? It was both disturbing and farfetched.

After much deliberation, they decided to go to the local Catholic Church, down in the valley and speak to Father De Melville. He was the head priest of St Patrick's church in town. He was originally from Kochi but had moved to Munnar more than sixty years ago. A benevolent man, he was a father figure to the town folk, and people of all faiths revered him. He was considered wise and trustworthy, and he held the utmost confidence of the people. Arvind and Demitri told him everything in detail, although they felt somewhat sheepish and embarrassed in doing so. The man of God, however, did not make light of their tale. He had heard every manner of stories and seen unbelievable occurrences, and would never casually dismiss anything, no matter how unusual or outlandish it seemed.

"Hmm!" That was the extent of his initial response! He stayed silent for a long time, but eventually said he could not make anything of it. He promised to ponder about and consult some of his close, wise and trusted associates without sharing any personal details and to keep it anonymous.

A couple of days later, Father De Melville reverted.

He said, "I'm afraid I have drawn a blank."

The two men, baffled and perturbed as they were, did not know to whom or where to turn.

The following morning, Arvind rose very early, dawn was still half an hour away. He felt a compelling need to clear his head, make some sense of all this illogicality, and see if he could fit the pieces of this jigsaw rationally without the surreal and the incredulous, with a mind free of emotional fog. A thick mist lingered in the lap of the emerald valley, and there was a distinct nip in the air. Arvind donned a thick, padded jacket; being a Mumbai boy, he was not accustomed to the cold. He also threw on a flat-topped, newspaper-boy type of twill cap on his head. Confused by the recent events and devoid of any answers, he stepped out and hoped that a long walk might help still his racy mind and lend clarity to his thought process and, who knows, provide him with some answers.

Soon he was more than a mile from the cottage. As he walked, he was lost in a world of his own. Unaware of his footfall or direction, he turned and followed random paths intuitively. He walked through the tea estates, from one well-worn foot path to another. So immersed was he in thought that he did not know in which direction he was headed or how much time had passed. When he did regain some self-awareness, he found himself in unfamiliar terrain. The tea gardens were left way behind – the hills had changed character. They were now covered with different vegetation and had flattened out a bit.

There was no sign of human life for miles around – just endless hills and some plains on the far horizon. Arvind had lost his bearings and had no idea where he was. He glanced at his watch; it was eight hours or more since he had left home and wandered this far unwittingly. It was afternoon now. He looked in every direction: far to his left, across the belly of a hill behind which the sun was just starting its journey to set for the day, he could see a tarmac road. It looked like a thin grey line drawn by a sharp pencil across the face of a hill. At the other end, he saw a lorry moving across on this road. It looked like a toy car. He thought getting to the road may well be his best bet of getting back to Munnar before sundown. He walked briskly in the direction of the road. It was much further than he had assumed, and it took him another hour of brisk walking to reach it. It was not the main route but in good condition and was solid tarmac.

Standing by the roadside, he looked both right and left, unsure which direction to take. He had left his trusted compass back at the annexe. He could toss a coin or just turn in either direction. Arvind took a deep breath, turned left, and started walking along the edge of the road. About half a mile down, he could see the faint silhouette of a milestone. He soon reached it and it read: Vagamon 103!

That was useful; at least he knew where this road was going. Vagamon was a town Arvind had never visited, and he knew that it was south; in fact, southwest of Munnar. approximately 100 kilometres. He realised he was headed the wrong way.

He turned around and started walking in the opposite direction. After a couple of kilometres of an arduous uphill climb, a faint whirring became audible, possibly of a motor engine approaching. Within five minutes, Arvind found himself sitting in the back of a small van, sharing the cramped space with about forty chickens being transported to Munnar to appease the appetite of tourists wanting their fill of poultry. The poor fowl had no way of knowing it was their last journey. He looked at their tiny, beady, restless eyes darting about, and they occasionally stared back at him. He was not sure if he imagined it or could see some fear in them.

That night was another restless one, and it was getting to be the norm. He was tossing and turning and kicking about with his restless legs, but at about two in the morning, he was suddenly wide awake, and he sat up and shouted out loud,

'Vagamon 103 – V 103! That's it!' he exclaimed, "That must be it!" He wanted to rush and tell Demitri but thought the Greek would not be pleased. It was strange his steps had carried him to that milestone. Was it a sign? Or a figment of his despairing imagination? He smiled and fell into a deep slumber.

The next day, the neighbour was once again woken up earlier than he would have liked, but with all that was going on, he expected it to be Arvind.

"Hello, Arvind!" he yawned as he spoke even before he had fully opened his front door. "What's up, neighbour?"

Arvind narrated his deduction of V 103, that he was confident that it is Vagamon 103.

"Really?"

"Do you think it is possible?"

"Hmm, I don't know, mie friend," said Demitri.

"But maybe worth exploring."

"Why don't we take a trip down to Vagamon; what's there to lose?" suggested Demitri with a grunt.

Arvind was quite surprised! Why hadn't he thought of that?

□

9

It was a bright Wednesday in early spring in Munnar. The hills looked handsome and majestic, green as envy. They were covered with a dense, undulating carpet of tea leaves. While humanity plays in the throes of joy and sorrow, triumph and disaster, pain and bliss, the stoic hills bear witness to the generations that come and go, accept every intrusion and insult without rejoinder unless their milieu is disturbed. Some generations hurt their soil, others provide balm and pamper the earth, which forever, only gives. The gods are also erratic in their empathy to them. Sometimes the rains are barely quenching, at others the slopes are awash with angry torrents. Fortunately, the hills always forgive and their song prevails.

Arvind and Demitri decided that it was a perfect morning to make the trip.

Demitri's only other significant possession besides the cottage and his so-called home-brew kit for wine making, but far more precious to him, was a 1967 Volkswagen Beetle. It was his pride and joy – the only thing he imported with him when he moved from Athens to Munnar. He had had it from new and was quite handy at looking after it. He had restored the engine himself many a time. Although he did not do much mileage these days, it read 258,000 miles on its odometer. It had lived the past few years of its life mostly sitting in his garage; he was often seen pottering or tinkering with it. Once in a while, you could hear it come to life. The engine would stutter, then cough and gurgle a few times, burst into a full-throttle, and off she would go down the country lanes, a canary yellow dot moving on the countryside, spouting greyish black fumes from its rear-loaded 1.6-litre engine. From afar, it looked like a smoking ladybird crawling across the hills.

After much debate, they had decided to head for Vagamon. The bug was all ready and loaded for a day trip. Arvind had to convince Demitri not to carry too much alcohol.

"My man, we are only planning a day trip, not a vacation to a 'dry' land for a month."

"It is for my mental wellbeing. As long as I know I have a good stock of this elixir of life, my soul breathes easier," responded Demitri.

The engine sputtered and spat, struggling to start. After seven attempts, the yellow bug finally came alive. The rear seats were occupied by much of Demitri's accessories, enough for a Himalayan expedition. The Beetle slowly made its way from his drive, on to the patchy country lane that led down from the cottage; the engine grunted a bit but managed to stay alive. A kilometre or so from the cottage, it met a recently laid tarmac road; a good quality road, thanks to the Kerala Tourism Board. They were doing their best to promote the tourism industry in these parts, much to the displeasure of those who wanted to preserve the tranquillity, quiet and relative anonymity still preserved in these hills. There is always a price to pay for so-called progress and development.

Munnar onwards, there were two possible routes they could choose from to reach Vagamon by road. The first was via Thodupuzha and Puliyanmala, and the second was via Kattappana and Kuttikkanam Road; the latter was about twenty kilometres shorter. The longer one was more picturesque. Since Demitri was in a good mood, he decided to take the scenic route. His Beetle could undoubtedly do with some much-needed exercise.

The purpose of the trip was primarily to check out

Vagamon and see if it offered any clues to the mystery playing out at the cottage and in their lives. They had no idea how or where to locate anything or anybody that may provide some answers. They were just following a hunch based upon Arvind's newfound theory of 'V 103'. They realised, that if they were to narrate their story and motives to anyone, it would make them seem like ghost chasers. They agreed to keep their theory between themselves. They still wanted to be considered 'sane'. It was a complete shot in the dark.

The road trip was its reward. The looping roads across the southern Western Ghats, the continuous roll of imposing hills, with enough green to paint the soul, was heart-warming. The route is dotted with small waterfalls all along. Many are mere trickles, some more full-bodied. These would be much fuller during the monsoon season, which was yet a few months away. Some mist was seen sprinkled across some of the hills in the distance, and an occasional drizzle greeted them every few kilometres as though it were a Benedictine shower. Arvind wondered if the rain was anointing their bravado or encouraging their naiveté. The Beetle's worn and warped wipers gnawed squeakily, yet barely cleared the windscreen. Demitri had to lean forward and strain to see through the condensation. They saw many trails plunging into the heart of the hills from off the main road. Motorcyclists, trekkers and hill-walkers often took these. Demitri knew that the Beetle would struggle on these, so he deliberately avoided them. It was a small miracle that the car was even roadworthy. They passed all kinds of foliage. Tea bushes flirted with the edge of the road where you could almost touch them. Patches of pine forests, seemingly out of place, were dispersed along the route. Many small lakes were visible from afar; some so small that they seemed just like a splash of blue paint dabbed accidentally on a green canvas. In the larger lakes, you could see honeymooners pedalling away blissfully in colourful pedal boats, often seen in such hill stations. Arvind had often wondered what was so romantic about pedalling a boat on a honeymoon.

There were innumerable potholes on the roads, wherever the tarmac had succumbed in patches under heavy rains. These, then, for the most part, had turned into puddles, some deep enough to make the Beetle's shock absorbers wail as the tyres dipped into them. Ice-cream vendors and picnic spots were scattered along the way. Key scenic view-points were sign-posted, hand-picked for the best photographs one could take as memories. Photography had become ubiquitous as everyone now had an efficient digital camera shoved into their back pocket. It was 'selfies galore', everywhere. Taxis full of tourists were starting to become more common even at this time of the year. An occasional backpacker could also be spotted, crawling up some slope. Every so often, there was a signboard for an Ayurvedic farm selling a promise of good health.

The Beetle hydroplaned and slithered a few times on the water-laden surface thanks to its balding tyres. At times it would almost hug the body of the hill, or skirt with the hem of the road on the valley side, tugging at the coat-tails of disaster but always managing to evade it. They stopped a couple of times to give the Greek a break. It was a challenge for Arvind to convince Demitri not to take a swig or two of his home-brewed tipples until they reached their destination.

Since they had no proper directions, a formal road map or satellite navigation in the relic of a car, they were dependent on the roadside signs, milestones, when legible and the odd pedestrian or roadside vendor. They still managed to lose their way a few times. About three hours into their journey, they finally came to a fork and were unsure which way to go. Demitri, being the eternally confident crusader, decided that the correct direction was towards the southwest. He swiftly turned left down an increasingly narrow, patchy road. After a mile, he started smacking his lips nervously as the road became narrower and more uneven. The bottom of the Beetle began grazing the ground now and again with a scraping noise. He also avoided Arvind's direct gaze boring down the side of his face.

"Are you happy with our presently chosen path?" asked Arvind with a hint of sarcasm.

"Yes, no!" he responded meaninglessly.

There was a thunderous noise as they passed a furious waterfall on the left. A few hundred yards later, they saw an old faded sign which read 'Kurisumala Ashram'. A smaller adjacent sign partly covered by an overgrown shrub read – 'Holymath Ashram'.

The Kurisumala Ashram at Vagamon was established in 1958 by the Benedictine monk, Francis Acharya. Its conception was in striking contrast to the spiritual activities and encroachments in the Idukki district during that period. Francis Acharya, the Cistercian monk belonging to the Benedictine congregation, was born in Belgium. At the ashram, Christian spirituality was interwoven with traditional Hindu practice. A large 'Om' was inscribed in the prayer room, a copy of the *Bhagavad Gita* sat alongside the Bible. There was a true amalgamation of religious thoughts and an east-meets-west approach. The secularisation of faiths, if possible, was the aim: One God for All.

The history of Kurisumala Ashram is also the history of the Acharya himself. He was born Jean Richard Mahieu in Ypres, Belgium. He had his early education and college studies in Brussels. At the age of twenty, he went to England for higher studies. While he was studying in London in 1931, he came under the influence of Mahatma Gandhi. Gandhiji had come for the Round Table Conference of the British Dominions, and had been contemptuously spoken of as a 'half-naked fakir'. Yet, in his simple Indian dress, he led the delegates into Buckingham Palace for an audience with Queen Mary. The nobility of his character and the simplicity of his life deeply touched Jean's heart. His influence inspired Jean to study the ancient culture of India. He began looking to it as the Land of Promise.

In September 1935, at the age of 23, Jean Richard joined the Cistercian Abbey of Our Lady of Scourmont, near Chimay,

Belgium. There he received a new name, Francis, with St. Francis of Assisi as his chosen patron. He took the solemn vows in 1940 and was ordained to the priesthood in 1941. At this time, the Abbot of Scourmont was planning to start a Cistercian monastery in India, which corresponded well with the aspirations of Father Francis. Somewhat later, the Abbot's interests began to turn more toward Africa. Nonetheless, Father Francis was permitted to undertake a foundation by himself in India. Father set sail for India and arrived in Bombay on 12 July, 1955. Swami Abhishiktananda welcomed him.

He travelled all over India to gain direct knowledge and experience of her people. He imbibed, quite readily, the spiritual nature of India through learning, travelling and seeking. He visited and stayed in many of the great ashrams of India.

In 1950, Abbe J. Monchanin (Swami Parama Arubi Ananda), a French missionary priest, and H. Le Saux (Swami Abhishiktananda), a Benedictine monk, had founded the Christian way of life on the bank of River Kaveri, near Trichy (Tiruchirappalli). Saccidananda Ashram, Shantivanam, was a Christian Ashram based on Indian spiritual tradition.

It was in 1955 that Zacharias Mar Athanasios, Bishop of Tiruvalla, a Syrian Catholic Church, invited Father Francis to make a monastic foundation in his diocese. Father Francis then came to Kerala for the first time. On 1 December, 1956, the two started the new foundation: Kristiya Sanyasa Samaj, Kurisumala Ashram at Tiruvalla in the Syro-Malankara Catholic Church. Eventually, they successfully obtained 88 acres of land. On 20 March, 1958, the eve of Saint Benedict's day, Father Francis, Father Bede, and two seminarians travelled sixty miles to the site high up on the holy mountain of Kurisumala. Well contented with their hilltop, they spent the next few months in a hut made of bamboo and plaited palm leaves with no facilities, no furniture, and a floor coated simply with cow dung. While the centre of their lives was the prayer of the Church and celebration of its feasts and mysteries, they had to find a way of supporting themselves, so they soon started a dairy farm with cattle imported from Jersey, England.

Soon, an English Benedictine monk offered to help them. They settled on the land and built a small monastery for twenty monks. Despite the isolation and quasi-inaccessibility of the place, the community counted another fifteen members within three years. At present, there are many more 'sanyasis', 'brahmacharis' and 'sadhkas'. Their life is a dedication to God and neighbour.

The most crucial feature of Kurisumala is its silence which pervades the Ashram. Gandhiji said, "Experience teaches that silence is the strength of all seekers of truth." These words of Gandhiji and the Indian monastic lifestyle prompted Acharya to give an important place to silence in the ashram. Guests who come from far and wide pray with 'The Harp of the Spirit'.

"What is this ashram business?" squealed a confused Demitri in a shrill voice.

"I think we took a wrong turn," he confessed as a couple of monks in ochre robes were walking towards us.

"Let's get out of heer," he whispered. Arvind clutched his forearm as he tried to turn the steering wheel.

"No, wait! Perhaps this is not an unexpected turn that you have taken. Maybe there is the hand of God here." Arvind tried to explain to him what an ashram is and its place in Indian culture.

"Rubbeesh!" replied Demitri, although there were plenty of Greek Orthodox monks and monasteries in his own culture and country. He had encountered many, and for the most part, his experience of them was positive even though he was an atheist. More monks were now walking past. They gave broad smiles and folded their hands simultaneously like Hindu people do when they greet somebody. *Namaste*!

"That is very interesting," Arvind thought aloud, given that they were Christian monks.

"Demitri, what do you say – since we have come this far that we go down and have a look at, what an ashram looks like from inside. We have nothing to lose, and afterwards, you could sip your 'sacred' wine, and I can drive us the remaining way down to Vagamon". He gave me a puzzled look, but being a good soul, he relented. In reality, it was the bribe and lure of the red elixir that had prevailed!

As they approached this famous ashram, they saw pastureland on both sides of the narrow road. Quite peculiarly, the breed of grazing cows was Jersey cows, and over thirty cows in a large enclosure; a small van had passed them earlier, it boldly displayed – 'KURISUMALA MILK' sign on its side. There were a few scattered goats and sheep also visible on the hillsides.

Demitri reluctantly agreed to see the ashram. When they reached the gate, two monks were standing guard at the entrance, who informed them that it was closed to visitors at this time because some part of the roof was under repair, scaffolding was visible. Both agreed to drive further down the lane to find a suitable place to turn the Beetle around and head into Vagamon town to find a place to spend the night.

As they went further on, about another mile or so, the road became narrower. Any scope of turning the car around was fading with every yard. To make things worse, the bottom of the Beetle was time and again scraping heavily against the dense gravel and grass path. It seemed to be struggling, and then quite abruptly, it grazed the turf with an intense screech and sputtered to a halt. Demitri was coming to the end of his tether, and he was about to let out some severe profanities when they both saw a sign, looked at each other and spoke out loudly in unison – "HOLYMATH ASHRAM!!"

They saw another bunch of monks attired differently from those of Kurisumala. They wore long saffron robes and smiled as they walked past. Demitri had stopped cursing his car by now, and we asked them if we could visit the ashram. The monks nodded in affirmation and gave us some directions. The entrance was only three hundred metres down the road.

We left the Beetle and walked towards the main building of the ashram. The envelope of green all around was overpowering. The ashram had thirty-eight acres to it. It was like a smaller Kurisumala.

"Are we in the right country?" continued Demitri. They passed a cheerful young boy who smiled from ear to ear and waved as he passed.

"This seems to be a land of milk, honey and happiness," quipped Demitri as another milk van passed.

Both felt a peculiar sense about this place.

□

10

Edoardo Leon Francesco, or 'Elf' as fondly nicknamed, was the head monk at the monastery-cum-ashram at Holymath for the last sixteen years. He was a tall, lithe, muscular man. He walked with the ease and slow grace of a gazelle and looked more like a long-distance athlete than an austere monk.

He had a rather intriguing past. Born the son of a pasta-maker in a village near Modena, Italy, he had worked shop since he could walk. His padre did not think much of schooling. He felt that the same curriculum for every child, who are all so different and unique, was pointless and led to the demise of both creativity and originality. He always said that we are filling the world with pathetic duplicates: clones.

Edoardo was an industrious child who worked from dawn to dusk with a perpetual smile, never complaining. Then at about the age of fourteen, his hormones kicked in, and boy – did they kick in! Edoardo rapidly lost interest in pasta-making; his life now focussed on rock and roll. His hair grew as rapidly as his facial features changed. He lost his baby fat, and developed into a handsome teenager, with rugged features; he let his hair grow to shoulder length. His life now was all about music; he spent all his time banging on his drum kit. He was so obsessed and persistent that his father almost turned him out of the house: ponytails and all!

Grandmother 'Mama' Alessandra, the head of the family,

was a powerful and strong-willed woman. If it wasn't for her, he could well have ended up homeless. She was tall, stern and fierce. Combine that with her name, which meant 'defender of mankind!' – a powerhouse personality – grandmother was a force to reckon with. She was the only one who could tell off this padre, who did not dare argue with her, as she would still smack him on the head if she had to!

She ensured Edoardo was assured of his place at home, supported his adolescent fad, and encouraged his musicality. He was the apple of her eye, and to her, he could do no wrong. In less than a year he became part of a local rock band. They started small and were soon playing gigs around Modena, to start with, but it wasn't long before they began to get bookings for events all over the region and within a few months, all across northern Italy. This process went on for a couple of years, and the band slowly but surely made a name for itself throughout the country and developed quite a cult following. During one such performance, a manager spotted the band while scouting for a recording label based in Milan: Ribo Records. He met the band backstage after the concert. After just a couple of meetings, the band had put their signatures on a recording contract.

Their first album went straight to number three on the Italian rock chart, and the second one to number one. Record sales soared, and Edoardo was suddenly famous, making a lot of money – more than he had ever imagined. He was on the cover of local magazines and a poster boy for teenage girls. With his newfound wealth, he lavished his grandmother with expensive gifts and poured out his love for her by spoiling her in every possible way. After all, if it hadn't been for her ... He bought himself all the usual fancy toys, including a bright red convertible Alfa Romeo – Spider by the time he was eighteen.

It was all going great guns, and it looked like Edoardo was on a long road to more fame and wealth. Their manager was planning a road trip with concerts all across Europe. Life was as good as it could be! One evening he was in Naples with his band, they were performing their biggest show ever at the Deigo Armando Maradona football stadium. Their music was riding a massive wave of popularity, and the venue was heaving with raving fans. Just when the band was on its fourth encore, back in Modena, Mama Alessandra had a massive heart attack, and took her last breath.

It was two days before Edoardo came to know. He was so profoundly stunned, he went into shock. He could not accept that he had lost his most precious grandmother so suddenly. He could not reconcile to this reality. It was as though life had been drawn out of his being. She meant the world to him. He got up from the band's dressing room and just walked out, away from it all, and left the band; against their wishes and requests. He dishonoured his contract even though he was committed to another two shows; one that very evening. He didn't care. She was the centre of his universe, which had just crumbled. She was only sixty-eight. What hurt him, even more, was that he never got a chance to say goodbye.

After her funeral for the next six days, Edoardo practically locked himself in a dark room. For ten days, he lived on water and some bread. Even he could not have imagined the impact that her passing would have on him. His grieving was intense, perhaps disproportionate, but when do we ever know the intensity of our love for another – how much, how deep it is and what they mean! Until we lose them.

As though an internal switch had flipped, Edoardo gave up his music. Everyone felt that this was an overreaction and a temporary phenomenon. Mama Alessandra was the one who had gifted him his first drum kit and then a guitar on his two consecutive birthdays at age eleven and twelve – she gave him the gift of music. It was as though he gave it all back to her. For once, his father backed off and did not say a single harsh word to Edoardo.

He changed completely. He was no longer the wild adolescent nor the prodigious musician. He became pensive. He withdrew and was silent most of the time, refusing even to meet his childhood friends. He would walk to Centro Evangelico Modenese Church every day, sit for hours in the pews and pray for his grandma's soul.

Here he ran into Father Bernardino, who was visiting Modena from Sicily on the business of his diocese. Father had observed this rather despondent boy who spent hours at a time in the church, day after day. He noted his sad countenance. On the fifth day, he came up to the young man and stood next to him. Edoardo looked up at this benign-looking face.

Father spoke without introducing himself and said, "Son, life is not for us to always make sense of; there is an unseen hand that shapes our destiny. Surrender and acceptance is sometimes the greatest wisdom. God be with you." With that, he walked back towards the altar. He was there for another three days before he was to leave for his monastery in Sicily. He never said another word to Edoardo. On his last day, Edoardo decided to go and speak to him – it turned out to be a pivotal conversation.

As he sat and listened to the man of God, he was amazed at the insight Father Bernardino had into life and how ignorant he was. Father was a catholic priest, but he honoured all the religions of the world. He had close ties with Buddhist monks in Vietnam, Vedic teachers in India, Shamanic priests of Mongolia, some Imams in Morocco and Sufi Derveshes in Cairo. He felt Christ was just one apostle of the Holy Spirit, the others were scattered all over the world. Some are known, but many others live in anonymity, burning an unseen but sacred candle of spiritual freedom, love and compassion.

Something churned inside him, and Edoardo unexpectedly realised that he had a different calling in life for the first time. He felt a resonance in his being, far more than he had felt about his music. A flame lit inside his being, and his eyes opened to an entirely new dimension of existence. He went home that day and seriously thought about his life and what he wanted to do. Having decided, he declared his intentions to his parents and family.

"I have decided that I am going to devote my life to the service of humanity," he said emphatically to a bewildered audience made up of his entire family, sitting around the dinner table the following night. They were dumbfounded – it was the last thing they would have expected from Edoardo. Under normal circumstances, his words would not be taken seriously and he would have incurred the wrath of his father. However, Edoardo sounded so serious and at the same time calm and filled with a firm conviction, that strangely his father sat silent. He was the only one who did not throw a classic Italian animated response.

"Are you going to become a priest or a monk?" asked one of his young cousins' she was only eleven-years old. Edoardo smiled. He had pondered long on his decision, staying up the previous night. He was convinced he had to take a particular path for his life.

He responded, "I do not want to become a priest and administer a confession or baptism, conduct marriages, anoint or bury people. Nor do I want to become a monk, as a man who has given his life to God living in a monastery under vows of stability, obedience and *'conversatio morum'*. I would like to lead a life of a humanitarian, guiding people towards the spiritual path rather than any religious doctrine."

In the meantime, his father had found his tongue and broke his silence, "And how do you intend to go about this?"

"Well, I have an invitation from Father Bernardino to spend some time at the diocese in Sicily. I will stay there for some time as claustral or lay brothers do. That is, until I find my path to fulfil my destiny."

"I shall be leaving in the morning at the first light," he said, dropping another bombshell quite casually. With that, he got up and left the dinner table and went back to his room. His family was left in a stunned and quasi-paralysed state. True to his word, Edoardo left at first light. He did not turn back, or he would have seen his father watching from a first-floor window with tears in his eyes.

He took a train down to the southern tip of Italy. It went via Bologna and Florence, the longest stopover being at Naples. In the matter of a few weeks, he had turned from a rock star to just another number on a passenger train. It was noon by the time they reached Naples *Stazione Centrale*. He was amazed at how busy it was. After what seemed like an age, the train eased out of Naples for the last leg of its journey. It was going to be another six hours, so he decided to get some sleep.

He woke with a sharp jerk when the train jingle-jangled loudly as it finally arrived at Reggio-Calabria. The Strait of Messina is a funnel-shaped arm of the sea that connects the Ionian Sea in the south to the Tyrrhenian Sea to the north. It is a small strip of water that separates mainland Italy from Sicily. At Reggio Calabria, after a series of jolts and groans, the train eased into the bowels of a large white ferry. Shortly, after the ferry left the port with the carriages on board, the passengers tumbled out of their bunks and seats and headed towards the ship's hold. It was like a well-rehearsed routine: they stepped around the back of the train and up to the bar where they ordered *arancino* and *vino,* and watched the lights of the mainland fade as they looked ahead in anticipation to see the lights on the shores of Sicily beckoning them.

Edoardo felt a mix of emotions as he looked back on his journey; he felt some thrill along with a sense of anticipation as he was stepping into an entirely new, unknown phase of his life. At the same time, there was a feeling of emptiness, as though he had forsaken something, but as is often with people who take a walk down this path, they have to sacrifice some part of their being. It's a lonely road, certainly not for the ordinary or faint-hearted, but those few moulded from a different clay. The price they pay seems worth it, to them. This new world he was stepping into couldn't be further from the throes of raving fans and wild tantrums of rock and roll. An alien and challenging life lay ahead of him.

He stayed for twenty months in Sicily; when he first arrived, he thought he would either quickly overstay his welcome at the monastery within a couple of months, or realise that this life was not for him. Contrary to his expectations, it turned out to be a rewarding experience. The monks and especially Father Bernardino took to him fondly. While there, he reverted to the non-complaining industrious child that he once was. He did most of the arduous work at the monastery, especially what no one else wanted he willingly accepted. He was the general dogsbody. His readiness to help everyone and natural mindfulness made him a much-loved resident.

During his stay, he grew sharply in his insight into this new world and its structure: a world of which most people know very little. It was a journey that only a handful can endure, and even fewer who may persevere. Even amongst those who choose to hold steadfast to it, only a handful can claim it to be their true calling. Edoardo was by no means a pushover who would be willing to accept anything said to him about God and the 'gateway to Heaven'. He had his deductions and perceptions of spiritual life and religiosity. However, he wisely never shared his personal opinion.

His time in Sicily passed swiftly. That fall, there was a visitor to the monastery, who had travelled from Kerala, India. Until that point, Edoardo had never heard of Kerala and only briefly of India, like so many people who live in the West, it was to him an exotic land of poverty, chaos, *yogis* and snake-charmers.

Krishnaswamy was his name; he turned out to be a simple but highly evolved and enlightened soul. Edoardo was taken by his simplicity. Swamy, as everyone called him, introduced Edoardo to the basic principles of Hindu and Buddhist spiritual philosophies – forbearance and non-duality. He learnt about devotion and surrender at an altogether different level, of non-violence and compassion, which were the fabric of these religions. However, a remarkable transformation was yet to happen. Swamy gave him a gift of an English translation of the excellent Hindu spiritual text, called the *Bhagavad Gita*. This ancient text is the fabric of Indian spiritualism, and it opened for Edoardo an entirely new vista of understanding the nature of existence and self-realisation. It kindled in him a new awakening and a deep yearning to visit this so-called spiritual land of the *yogis*.

Two months later, he embarked on 'AURORA', a ship sailing from Genoa to India; the long voyage made its only stop for half a day at Palmera, to collect some supplies. As he stood on the deck with the warm sea breeze caressing his face, he could feel an excitement within him, merely at the thought of reaching Kochi, on the east coast of India, off the Bay of Bengal twenty-seven days later.

He couldn't wait to see India!

□

11

India was an invasion of his senses in every sense of the word. He was astounded by this crazy cauldron of sights, sounds, colours, aromas and visions, as much with her high standard and prevalence of spiritual undercurrent and religiosity. However, to begin with, he could not understand the need for a thousand different gods. This was typical of all foreigners who travel to India and seem confused and disgruntled by the number of gods and goddesses available for worship. Little do they realise that it is merely choice that is varied and that Indians clearly understand that there is but one God and they are free to worship him by whatever name they please – be it a tree, a snake, a monkey or an elephant! It was just another means of endorsing the oneness of the divine.

He realised quicker than most visitors that they were all worshipped under the same premise. It was evident to him that divinity remained ubiquitous and omnipotent for people of this subcontinent. He travelled the length and breadth of the country for three years, spending a good deal of time meditating in the foothills of the Himalayas. During this time, he also visited numerous ashrams, met sages and *yogis*, heard their discourses with an open mind. He even endured so-called 'godmen', many self-proclaimed and fake, for the sake of his clarification and spiritual growth. He was sometimes amazed and at others, bewildered at what he encountered. He felt sad and concerned for the innocent ones duped by those cloaked in ochre or white robes, a mere mask on their religious falsehood. He remained unfazed and unimpressed by them.

Religion in India was without doubt 'the opium of the people'. However, it was all part of the varied tapestry of this unique land. He was willing and able to sieve through the fake and the pretentious, along with the bigots, impersonators, seducers, and debauches. Over the first few months, he developed enough insight to know the difference.

The dichotomy between the rich and poor did eat into his heart and mind. There was a high prevalence of illiteracy which he thought was a key issue in the making of a weaker society. Equally, he realised that being literate was over-rated; beyond a certain point, education or qualifications were unrelated to leading a righteous life. Going to college did not necessarily, lend itself, or equate to being learned. He encountered many poor, uneducated people who had deep wisdom and understanding of life. They were virtuous and happier, more balanced and joyous than their so-called educated counterparts. Also, he had encountered and dealt with many upper- and middle-class Indians who, on the one hand, were fluent in the Queen's English and behaved like the polished elite; on the other, were crooked, crude and morally bankrupt. Perhaps modern society and its parameters were holding on to the wrong end of the stick.

One particular experience influenced him profoundly. It occurred during Edoardo's Himalayan wanderings. At one point he was up in the hills of Himachal Pradesh in northern India and headed for Rohtang Pass, when there was an unseasonal and unexpected, heavy and prolonged snowfall. He was forced to take a detour which happened to be through the valley of Spiti. The name 'Spiti' means 'The Middle Land', i.e. the land between Tibet and India, nestled in the lap of the Himalayas. This was a real find for Edoardo: so much for the hand of destiny.

Spiti is a cold desert valley with the pristine Spiti river

flowing through its bosom. Stark and barren, yet picturesque mountains surround it on either side, and the river is like a blade of blue steel bisecting the valley. The hills are adorned with a staccato of dotted houses and a couple of monasteries. The valley is a research and cultural centre for Buddhists. There were two monasteries – Key Monastery and Tabo Monastery. A good majority of the population there followed Buddhism: a religion born out of the womb of Hinduism but follows a somewhat different path to enlightenment. He remembered Father Bernardino talking to him about Buddhist thought. The bad weather turned out to be a blessing in disguise as he sought shelter at the Key Monastery. He had planned on staying overnight to ride out the blizzard, but remained there for more than three months. It was pure serendipity.

He was profoundly influenced by the monks he met at the monastery. They gave him further insight and outlook into the spiritual realm. Spiti was the icing on the cake of his spiritual quest. It put a seal of affirmation to his thought and search. The detour was a boon to Edoardo. He was now three years into his Indian travels and finally felt that he had gained enough foresight about the direction he wanted to take for his future life. However, he was unsure how he would accomplish this; but now he held no fear. Like the unexpected encounter with Spiti, he felt that his life would open other doors by itself.

With that thought affirmed in his being, he made his way back to where he had first stepped on to Indian soil, Kochi. As he boarded the train from Shimla in the south of the state, he realised this could be his last journey on the Indian Railways. He considered it a matter of just forty-three hours. He was ready to return to his motherland, Italy.

Rail journeys in India are as exhausting as they are exhilarating, and a person may experience an intense snapshot of life simply on one such trip. There is on display: colours, sights and sounds beyond one's imagination. People's food, weather, appearance, and dialect change every eighty kilometres, yet the human factor remains the same. There is joy, laughter, tears, sorrow, grief, hunger, waste, luxury, turmoil, peace. Compassion, anger, kindness, humility, theft, poverty, riches, brotherhood, loneliness, family love, mourning and celebration – all served on the same plate in a single journey if only one had the eyes to see and the heart to feel the tapestry of an entire culture laid bare. That is why travels in India are such a potent concoction. He decided that for a few days he would stay in the town where he first set foot into this revered land before he left for Italy. He had come a full circle. He felt the pull of his country intensifying inside him, confident that he would soon be on his way home.

On his last evening in Kochi, the day before he was set to sail for the Adriatic, he visited the local Anglican Church with which he was familiar. He had frequented it when he first arrived in Kochi, and he wanted to say goodbye to Father Brown, who was a priest there. He entered and walked towards the altar. As he approached, he noticed a man standing with his back to him, stooped in posture. He was wearing the white robes of a priest. He turned around as he heard footsteps. To Edoardo's utter surprise, the person he last expected to see standing before the altar was Father Bernardino! He looked like an apostle of peace. Father himself seemed less surprised and Edoardo wondered why. All was revealed soon enough. Father Bernardino had been keeping track of Edoardo's whereabouts for the last year and had come to know from friends in Spiti that Edoardo would be returning to Kochi, so Father had come to meet him.

After an uncharacteristic and warm embrace, as Edoardo knelt to kiss his hand, he spoke, "Edoardo, I have come here for a specific purpose. We have been allocated some land up in the hills of Kerala, about a hundred kilometres from here, and the diocese intends to set up a new monastery." He paused and took a shallow breath.

"I am too old to start a project of this magnitude. From the first moment we met, Edoardo, I felt a spark in you, an uncompromising passion, and a spirit seeking a deeper meaning and path. Also, I know that you are not dogmatic about any one particular religion. Here in India, this becomes especially important. Spirituality runs in the veins of the people, albeit unbeknownst to them. India is the land of sages, and there is untold wisdom in this culture. Enlightenment is given the highest accolade, even above godliness. I am confident that you have a clear understanding of this fact, given your time here. I think the time has come to amalgamate religious freedom with spiritual unity. I have always felt that there should be a fresh approach towards worship and devotion.

"With this in mind, I have waited here for you. I would be pleased and at peace, if you accept the reins of this special gift and opportunity that we have. Indeed, I also think this is the best way forward for you, and this could become tremendous labour of love for you, and in return, it will be a blessing for the local and greater community and a favour to the diocese."

He paused when he saw Edoardo who had been taken by surprise, though listening intently was still trying to take it all in.

"What do you think?"

Edoardo remained silent. It was quite a daunting proposal and most unexpected. He knew that his mentor was a man of great wisdom and depth, and felt very grateful that Father had even considered him for such a project. It was a great honour. Nonetheless, he was unsure if he could take on such a huge responsibility.

He took a long time and then slowly knelt and kissed the signet ring on Father Bernardino's right hand, as the latter leaned forward, smiled and embraced him.

The following week Edoardo left for the hills of Idukki in a rickety old Ambassador taxi. He carried his meagre belongings, a box full of books and some information leaflets about the diocese and official government documents relating to the allocated land.

Throughout the journey, his mind was wrestling with

various possibilities. What could he do? How would he create a new dimension about how people could worship? That too, in this land which is so steeped in its dogmatic beliefs. Father Bernardino had given him a free hand and his blessings. His directions were simple and very much in sync with Edoardo's new thinking. He wanted to create a unique place, a haven, something more than a monastery – an 'ashram' – a place where the strict divide of religions would dissolve. Where the Christians would welcome and stand alongside the non-Christians. The margins of faith would be blurred and, instead, there would be a mutual spiritual awakening of humankind.

That was the beginning of the Holymath Ashram!

□

12

Demitri and Arvind pushed the Beetle to one side of the thick grass verge. They saw some plain and rusted iron gates in front of them. A small discrete sign carved in wood, with painted white borders and almost hidden by an overgrowing jasmine hedge stated the name of the ashram – Holymath. Arvind liked that it was not ostentatious. On Demitri's firm push, the gates opened with a low-pitched creak. As soon as they entered the compound, they felt unfamiliar energy – an immediate ambience of stillness and tranquillity.

Demitri's countenance changed instantly. He acquired a look that Arvind had never seen before. He seemed calm and bewildered simultaneously, and his typical fidgety nature disappeared. They walked in silence towards the main building of the ashram. Both felt a strange sense of anticipation, for which there was no explanation.

The doors to the main ashram building were ordinary. Arvind stepped forward and rang the doorbell. A benevolent-looking monk with a genial smile on his face, wearing light, faded, burgundy-coloured garments appeared at the door.

"Hello!" he said in a musical tone. "What can I do for you gents?"

Demitri was the first out of the blocks, "Err, em, we just wanted to have a look around," he said, trying not to sound nosey.

"Most certainly. Would you care to step in?" said the monk, flashing a warm smile!

They both removed their shoes and stepped into a dim-lit hall. They immediately felt a sense of serenity and calm. The dwellings were meagre and simple. There was no display of wealth here as often seen in temples, especially in India, where deities are bathed with milk and honey and adorned with gold and jewels. It was apparent that the approach to worship was different here. There were a few wall hangings with spiritual quotations, and an occasional landscape painted in water colours. Photographs of various Bishops of the Diocese, who had served over the years, hung along one long stretch of a wall. They followed the monk around the thinly-carpeted floor towards the main altar. There were a handful of monks dressed similarly, sitting in mindful contemplation. The altar was simple, with a cross in the centre made from either pewter or white metal, and there was nothing ornate about it. On the right side of the wall, Arvind noted an OM inscribed in the centre of what seemed to be an old coat of arms.

Demitri thought that perhaps things were a bit too plain and dull.

Just then the monk asked, "Would you like to see the outdoors?"

He then opened a flimsy side door, and the three of them stepped out. It was as though the doors to a magical garden had been unlocked: a fantastic scenery opened before them. There was an endless, panoramic view of acres upon acres of handsomely landscaped hills, interspersed with tea estates and pretty gardens. Even though Demitri and Arvind lived in a very picturesque setting, this view was something else! There were patches of wild flowers, grazing land, well-manicured gardens and some dense forests. Stone trails led down to some of these forested areas. The variety of trees was incredible; there were junipers and eucalyptus interspersed with conifers and *gulmohur* (flame of the forest). They could also see three waterfalls. The whole view was as though somebody had rolled out a majestic multi-coloured carpet woven with nature. It was indeed a Garden of Eden!

"Feel free to walk around, rest, and spend as much time here as you please. I will be inside if you should need me. My name is Mohan."

He turned and left them to their own devices. For the next forty minutes or so, they both wandered about this idyllic paradise. They did not speak at all: when one is in the lap of Mother Nature, words can be unnecessary. After a while, they both sat down in silence on a rustic wooden bench that allowed a beautiful view of the hills before them

"I could stay here forever," Demitri said, finally breaking the silence and letting out a heavy sigh. Arvind had never seen this side of Demitri ever before.

An hour or so later, Mohan returned and told them more about the place. Holymath was still managed by Father Edoardo, who was now about sixty-eight years old and had built the monastery from scratch. It was his labour of love; his life was dedicated to it.

The side door opened, and a grey-haired gentleman in a white robe stepped out towards them. He had a thick, rope-like cincture around his waist, the hanging tassels of which gently bobbed back and forth with each step he took. He had a broad stole, hemmed with thin red thread, around his shoulders. A black onyx cross on a silver chain hung low from his neck on his amice.

"That is Father Edoardo," said Mohan, as he made a slight courtesy-like gesture and left them. Father strode towards them. He had sparse silver hair and walked with the gentle, effortless grace of a puma. He was slim and tall, with dark bronzed ageless skin, and his eyes seemed to embody compassion. He looked sagacious.

"Hello," said Father with a warm smile.

Both Demitri and Arvind responded, "Hello" in unison. Demitri, all this while, was trying to suppress an urge to embrace the man. Such was Father's persona that it imbued these feelings in him.

"What brings you two gentlemen to Holymath?"

Without a second thought, Arvind narrated the whole story and the chain of events that had prompted this trip. Father Edoardo's reaction was far from anything they would have expected from anybody who heard this ridiculous-sounding tale and course of events. But he seemed to take it all in as though he believed every word that Arvind uttered. He kept silent for a while and then responded, "In my life and travels, I have seen and experienced so many implausible events and heard incredible stories that yours does not surprise me! There are so many occurrences far above and beyond the dimensions of normal human perception and understanding.

"I sense there is certainly something deeper here. I can completely understand your quest to find an answer. I also have a feeling that it may well lead you to more unexpected shores," he said quickly and spontaneously. This was least expected by both of them.

The side door of the ashram building opened and a young lad stepped out towards them. A faint smile immediately appeared on Father Edoardo's lips. The boy walked briskly towards the three of them with a slight skip in his step. His face bore a wide brimming grin.

He was instantly likeable.

□

13

Madhav was a charming, shy, country boy who looked a tad underweight. He was tall and thin, with shiny white buck teeth, displaying a disarming smile that seemed to be permanently pasted on his face. He had dimples on his cheeks, and even his large beady eyes carried a spark of happiness. A tiny pewter cross hung from a black thread tied tightly around his neck. He reached them quickly, given his long strides, and looked lovingly at Father Edoardo. Father placed a gentle arm across his shoulders and introduced him with a tinge of pride in his voice, "This is Madhav, the youngest resident at our ashram. As you might know, children are not allowed here and cannot be inducted into monkhood until they are sixteen; he is just over ten years old."

He continued, "The circumstances of his arrival here were rather bizarre. It was just over ten years ago on a very dark, moonless night. We had just completed our evening prayers and sermon when we heard a distant but clear sound. A sound we had never heard before at the ashram. The nights here are notably silent. It sounded like the stifled cry of a hungry kitten. We traced it down to the main gate, and were startled by our find. Wrapped in a thin muslin cloth lay this child, just a few hours out of his mother's womb. When we reached him, there was a beautiful smile on his face; no sign of any tears! We looked around, but there was nobody to be seen, no sign of his mother or any other person. We immediately dispersed all our monks in various directions to see who could have left him at the monastery gates, but there was no one to be found even after a very exhaustive search. Nobody had seen or was aware of a woman with a babe in arms seen in the vicinity or a few miles' radii of the ashram.

"It would typically be against the monastery's rules or those of the Diocese to adopt or keep a baby, but somehow, it never occurred to us to take him down to the local orphanage. All the monks were keen to keep him with us, especially after our search for a parent returned empty-handed, and the way we found him seemed like an injunction from the Lord himself. Uncharacteristically, even I did not raise any objections. He seemed like a gift.

"I sent people the following day into the local townships and hospitals, nursing homes and villages, to check on the children born in the past couple of days. All the births were accounted for, and no one could provide us with any relevant information. Even the local midwives could not give us any leads. Well, we simply kept him. He has been the most amicable child one could have and is the life and light of this place, loved by everyone, and even the local town-folk and occasional visitor such as you. He is a bit of a mascot now. I call him '*Figlio da fortuna*' – the son from fortune.

"There was one strange occurrence, though: Madhav did not speak till he was eight-years old, not a word! He could hear everything, and, in fact, he had better hearing than a moth. There also seemed to be no issue with his intelligence or comprehension, yet he would not utter a single word. We spoke to a few doctors who could not suggest much, given his normal hearing and development. Then, at eight years old, down to the day we found him, one night he wandered away from the ashram: we kept looking for him for two days, but we could not find him. He returned by himself with a big smile on his face and a vocabulary and speech that would put any other eight-year old to shame. Since that day we cannot stop him, and he has been a chatterbox. Another of the Lord's miracles."

All this while what went unnoticed was that Madhav had his gaze transfixed on Arvind, and tears were streaking down his cheeks like trickling raindrops. It was only when Father Edoardo paused to take a deep breath that he noticed this. They were all taken aback. In all these years that Madhav had been at the ashram, nobody had ever seen him cry or be gloomy, even if he had a passing ailment, fever, or felt unwell. If he hurt himself running up the hills or skinned his knees climbing trees, he was the most unaffected child and never cried. But today, completely unprovoked, the floodgates had opened.

Father Edoardo was truly bewildered, and he could not help notice Madhav's constant gaze towards Arvind.

"What is the matter, Madhav?" asked Father softly as he embraced the child. Madhav merely shook his head while the tears still flowed. Arvind was also astounded by what had just happened. He could not understand why he was staring at him and crying. He had never travelled to this area previously and never met this child. He had tutored quite a few children in Munnar, but he had never left Munnar since he had first arrived there over two years earlier. Madhav shook his head and buried it into Father's robe.

In the meantime, it started raining and gathering pace, so Father suggested that they go inside the monastery. They all went in and sat down at a vast, chunky, rectangular dining table made of Indian rosewood. One of the younger monks brought some tea, biscuits and sweets made from the local Kurisumala milk. By this time, Madhav's wailing had quietened down to a mere whimper, but he was still not fully pacified.

Father himself became quite pensive. Being quite an evolved soul himself through years of spiritual practice, he did not take things at face value and was confident there was a deeper undercurrent to what had just happened. However, he did not say anything. The evening was drawing close, and Father Edoardo spoke to Arvind and Demitri without addressing Madhav's outburst.

"It does not look likely that the rain will stall for the next few hours. These are not very good conditions for you to drive out of here as the roads are slippery and can be risky. If you gentlemen would like, you are most welcome to stay the night here at the ashram and leave once the weather settles down. We are used to having regular visitors, and a couple of guest rooms are always prepared."

They both readily agreed.

Arvind and Demitri were both shown a room. They exchanged bewildered glances, as soon as they entered, and Demitri blurted half-accusingly, "What the hell did you do to that poor child?" sounding like his old self.

Arvind responded, still a bit shook up, "I am puzzled about that myself!!"

There were both quite exhausted by their journey and quickly fell asleep. Arvind must have slept only for a couple of hours when he awoke. It seemed that there was a raging thunderstorm outside, only to realise that it was the roaring snore coming from Demitri. The rain was a mere pitter-patter by now.

He knew that there was little or no chance of getting any more sleep given the hundred-decibel volume of the snoring. He sat up in bed and considered the events of that afternoon and evening. He thought about the intensity with which the boy had cried and the pathos in his eyes; also the way Madhav's gaze had held him was inexplicable. Arvind felt decidedly uncomfortable that he had evoked such a response without having done or said anything, especially when he had thought the boy was so pleasant. What could have overwhelmed him?

He decided to step out; so donned a light jacket and went out through the side door. The rain had almost stopped. He walked through the gardens adjacent to the monastery. The ambience was serene, especially as the full moon had started to peer out from behind the breaking clouds. Soon the rain stopped completely, and the green around him turned to a silvery turf bathed in moonlight. He walked close to the main building of the ashram as he did not know his way around.

It was then that he heard the faint sounds of the tappets of a typewriter – 'Chick-a-chik'!

Arvind froze, 'You have to be kidding me! Not here too?' he muttered to himself. But the sound was unmistakable, although much softer than the sound he heard at the cottage. He thought it was his imagination. What were the chances of another similar Remington typewriter being present here and going off in the middle of the night? He thought he was turning neurotic! Had his neighbour not been a witness to all that had elapsed, he would have had to consider the option of a straitjacket.

The sound died quickly and did not return. Arvind decided to return to the room and thought he would not mention this to anyone, including Demitri, as he would undoubtedly be declared insane! He convinced himself that it was his mind playing tricks on him.

Despite the ballistic snoring of his friend lying next to him, Arvind eventually slipped into an uneasy sleep. His dreams were vivid, with tormenting visions of floating demons, huge dragons and evil spirits in brightly painted veils, and tempest seas with ships tossed about like twigs. He was very restless. However, the last dream he had was of his daughter smiling, waving at him and clapping her hands and blowing kisses at him. He woke up with that image still lingering before his eyes.

The morning brought with it sparkling sunshine from a cloudless sky. Leaves still held up tiny dewdrops, and it looked like nature had sprinkled pearls on them. The monastery had been long up, the morning prayers were done, and these devoted early risers had already accomplished most of the day's tasks. Mohan gently knocked on their door. He said he would arrange their breakfast and once they were done eating, Father Edoardo said he would like to meet them before they went on their way.

Demitri and Arvind finished a wholesome but simple

breakfast. Demitri still seemed a bit sedated and Arvind contemplative. Once they had some tea, they told Mohan they were ready to meet up with Father. He was standing in his small office, looking out of the window at the valleys and hills. He turned slowly to face them as they came into the room. From his somewhat drawn face, it seemed that he had not had a very restful night either.

"Gentlemen, please sit," he gestured to them. Father paused, drew in a deep breath. "As you can imagine, this is a rather disturbing and perplexing matter for me, to see the child break down as I have not seen in the last ten years that he has been with me. I have raised him more watchfully than I would a son, given that he has never met his mother and that we don't know who his parents are. We are his family. Hence, I know that this is very much out of character for him." He paused, "I have spoken to him. He said that he does not know what happened, but it was definitely after he saw Arvind that something inside him just gave way. He cannot explain anymore; it was as though there was something, a ... a connection from somewhere. As you told me, you are from Mumbai and have only been in Munnar for the last two years or so. This means when Madhav was found at our gates, you were more than a thousand kilometres away, so there is no way to link the two of you?

"Yet your story also relays some very unusual, if not paranormal series of events that have brought you to Vagamon and Holymath. It seems that you have almost been led here. It does seem surreal. Having seen much in this life, I wonder if there is some unusual explanation for all this.

"Dr. Arvind, is there anything you could tell me about your life, even trivial or unusual as it may seem, which could help us in explaining Madhav's outburst? Please understand that you are not obliged to do so: it also feels quite bizarre and absurd to ask you for this, and I would fully understand if you were to decline my request."

Arvind responded in a way that even surprised him,

"Father, this incident has taken a huge toll on me too. As I mentioned to you, my daughter was very precious to me, and she would have been near about the same age that Madhav is. Also, I can see in him a delightful and pure child. I am fully willing to tell you whatever you wish to know, and share any information that could explain this peculiar occurrence."

"Please tell me about your late wife and daughter, everything that you feel you can share," urged Father Edoardo, sounding very solemn and respectful After all, he was a priest.

Arvind started from the time he met Anamika, including their courtship and wedding. He then spoke about her pregnancy, his medical career, their beautiful daughter and enviable life, how the extortion and threats began and, after that, the tragic accident they had met with.

"How and why did you come to Munnar, Dr. Arvind?"

"Father, please don't address me as Dr. Arvind; just Arvind would be fine. Believe it or not, Father, that is still a mystery to me, but I can certainly recount for you the events as they occurred."

Arvind took a deep breath and swallowed hard to clear the lump that was quickly welling up in his throat, "For the next few days after I lost my wife and daughter, I was in a daze. I went through the funeral and mourning ceremonies like a zombie, alive but numb: inside me was a dense fog of disbelief and shock. Once all the clamour around the accident died down, and the deluge of friends and relatives had dwindled, I was left alone with my sorrow and loneliness, empty and broken.

"Both sets of parents were trying to be as supportive as possible, but I felt smothered by their affection. Nothing was helping.

"After a few weeks, my friends, patients, and other relatives stopped visiting. The phone calls dried up. I am sure they felt that I was unredeemable, and, to be fair, I refused to engage or communicate with them. People offer compassion and advice, but that, somehow, does not give you any meaningful solace.

Nobody seemed to understand that this was a storm I could not weather. Of course, I never returned to my clinic. I told my family to make arrangements to sell off my clinic for whatever they deemed appropriate. That happened quite quickly. The police investigation drew a blank. I was in a very dark place and inches away from ending it all. Then I don't know what happened. One day I decided it was the end of the road for me. I left home with a substantial sum of money and started walking. I had no idea where I was bound or what I was about to do, and there was no plan, no destination." Arvind paused as a tear rolled down his cheek.

The two other men could feel his grief. Demitri placed a gentle hand upon his shoulder. Though the two men were friends and met almost daily, they had never delved or pried into each other's past or private lives.

Arvind drank some water offered by Father and continued, "I walked aimlessly for a few hours and found myself facing the Chhatrapati Shivaji Terminus. Father, you may know this as VT or the Victoria Terminus, and you may also be aware, this is the main railway station of Mumbai. I must have stood in front of it for I don't know how many hours, staring at its marble Gothic façade with eyes that saw nothing and a heart that felt empty, unaware of the thousands of passengers that passed by – they were invisible to me.

"Around midnight, I found myself walking into the station. I could see a train standing in front of me on platform No 1. I walked up to the first ticket counter and asked the attendant which was the next train scheduled to depart. He told me it was the delayed 'Kochuveli Express', and I bought a second-class ticket for the last stop. I got on the train and found a dark, quiet corner in one of the coaches, sat down and stayed put. Quite honestly, it was all a bit of a blur. The journey takes typically about twenty-six hours to reach its final destination. I am uncertain how long it took to get there as I had no cognition of time; I don't think I ate or drank at all during the whole journey. I had to be physically coerced off the carriage by the cleaners at the railway yard at Kochuveli. I walked out in a trance. Right across the street, I saw the Kerala State Road Transport Corporation's inter-state bus terminal. I again stepped on to the first bus leaving and again asked for a ticket to the last stop. It was destined for Munnar. That is how I got there, and after that never left till yesterday."

All three of them sat in silence for some time while Arvind gathered himself.

Then Father said, "You said something about an incident that occurred during the middle of your wife's pregnancy when you were narrating the story of what led you to Vagamon?"

"Yes, Father. Anamika had a pregnancy with identical twins to start with, but somewhat unexpectedly mid-pregnancy, one foetus, so to speak, disappeared. It was considered a rather unusual phenomenon even by the obstetricians. Why do you ask?"

"What was your daughter's date of birth?"

"6th May, 1996," replied Arvind.

Father turned slightly pale, "That was the very same day we found Madhav at the gates of the ashram, and he would have also been born the same day!"

They all looked mystified. Demitri was looking blanched.

"Sorry to rekindle old wounds, but what was the date she was taken away by the Lord?" asked Father.

"17th May, 2004."

"That was the day that Madhav suddenly started to speak; until then, not a squeak came out of him!"

"What ... what ... !" butted in Demitri.

"This is unreal! What a strange coincidence!" added Father.

Arvind said, "I must mention something that I was not going to but, considering the turn this conversation has taken, I must. Father, do you recall we mentioned the typewriter incident to you yesterday? Well, last night, while I had wandered into your gardens, I heard the same sound again, although briefly. I am sure it was not a figment of my imagination!"

Born on the same day as Mehak? Started talking the same day as Mehak died? It was unreal. There was no way to make sense of it. However, if you add on to this the way Madhav had reacted to Arvind, and the whole absurdity around the typewriter, being virtually led to Vagamon by strange events. They were all a bit dumbfounded!

At this point, Father Edoardo had fallen silent and become introspective and inflective. They all waited patiently for him to say something. The cat had got Demitri's tongue much earlier, and Arvind was visibly disturbed. After what seemed like an eternity, the silence was broken by Father.

He said, "I have, within the realm of my own life, experienced and witnessed many mysterious things, some bordering and others immersed in the supernatural. I have seen and known mystics with super-human powers and *yogis* that are in communion with the spirits of people who don't even exist any longer. It is also well enshrined in history that some people who have left this earth in unexpected or sudden and inexplicable circumstances have sometimes still lingered in some way or form.

"We have all heard of some children who can recall details of their past life, even identify the people and villages, and in the homes, they had lived. Crazy as it may seem, I think we need to look at this matter closely and delve deeper and explore. Let's see if there is something in it or it is just an unusual coincidence. If this was not playing out in the domain of our personal experience, we might not have considered this a possibility. Especially knowing Madhav the way I do, it might be worth speaking to him. I shall do this tomorrow; better to give him some time to settle down a bit."

He suggested to Demitri and Arvind that they were welcome to stay another couple of days at the monastery and explore the local region if they wished to. He would spare a monk to show them around and familiarise them with the activities of the ashram. They could partake in these if they so wished. They both nodded in solemn acceptance.

Over the next two days, they savoured the sights and sounds of the hills and valleys surrounding the monastery in the cantankerous Beetle, with a monk in tow. The monk showed them views of exceptional natural beauty. They soaked themselves in the serenity and wonder of this green valley as they roamed the many trails around. But it wasn't quite the experience it seemed, considering the recent events.

Demitri appeared quite engrossed in the spellbinding beauty of the boundless nature around them, but was no longer his old self. Arvind was in turmoil inside: he could not overcome the impact of recent events, the image of that tearful boy staring at him through pining eyes that never left him. It was as though he was staring right at his soul.

What was the connection? All this seemed like a surreal and supernatural coincidence. His subconscious was shuddering with swathes of inexplicable retort. As a man of science, he was not able to accept any supernatural explanation. Nevertheless, the recent chain of events of the last few years had made him sceptical about the rational and scientific nature of his existence.

He was coming to a point where he was willing to believe anything. Was he clutching at straws, trying to sew shreds of his beloved daughter into a garment that he could wear to pacify his soul? He did not know what was happening.

Two days passed. Arvind was present physically, but his mind was stuck in constant analysis, and the nights were a torment. On the third day, Father Edoardo caught up with them. He still looked drawn. He drew a deep breath and spoke, "Arvind, I have been speaking to Madhav, and he has no further insight into this episode. After much cogitation, I feel that I would like Madhav to spend more time with you if you are agreeable. I understand it may not be feasible for you to stay here much longer. Is it possible for Madhav to visit you in Munnar?"

Demitri chipped in quickly, "If Arvind is happy to do so,

then Madhav could return to Munnar with us and spend a few days. I have a spare room in my cottage, and he could stay as long as you like."

Father looked at Arvind. It was quite an unexpected request as far as Arvind was concerned. Amid all these confused ruminations, he had not considered this option. He paused for thought and concluded that it could not do any harm. He nodded in affirmation. Father had already spoken to Madhav before raising this issue with Arvind.

The apprehension in Madhav's eyes was apparent to Father, but somehow it had not taken much persuasion to get him to agree.

□

14

The morning brought forth another striking day to Vagamon. Madhav climbed into the back seat of the Beetle, sharing the space and dwarfed by Demitri's mountain of accessories. He clutched tightly on to his small shoulder bag in which he had enough clothes for a couple of days. They left early by Demitri's standards, just after nine. Madhav was quiet throughout, and Arvind did not have much to say. Demitri tried to create an amiable, even mirthful atmosphere; however, he could feel the constant gaze of the child burning into his back.

They made it back up to Munnar without a hitch, although Arvind's back was sore – the Beetle had the suspension of a bullock cart! As they entered Munnar, Madhav started getting a bit fidgety. When he saw the cottage from afar, he spoke for the first time, "Is that where we are going?"

"Yes," replied Demitri.

The Beetle was weary by now, and its engine started shuddering and sputtering as it went uphill towards the cottage. Unhealthy flumes of charcoal-coloured smoke was spewing out from the exhaust pipe in large clouds. Arvind was not sure it would make it to the cottage, and so it turned out. About three hundred or so yards before the cottage, the engine died.

"Oh, dear!" said Demitri. He repeatedly tried to crank the

engine, but it was dead as a doormat.

"Never mind, we are not too far from home," observed Arvind. They all got off and trudged towards the cottage. As they neared it, Demitri placed one hand on Madhav's shoulder and said to him, "That is where I live, and there is a spare room for you."

By this time, Madhav's eyes were getting a bit frantic and his pupils dilated a bit. They were darting from side to side as though searching for something. About a hundred yards short of the cottage, he broke into a sprint towards and stopped right in front of the door of the annexe.

Demitri shouted from afar, "It's the other door on the opposite side!"

But Madhav did not budge and kept staring at the annexe door. By this time, they had caught up with him. His restlessness was turning into a minor agitation. Arvind and Demitri exchanged bewildered glances. Arvind unlocked the door to the annexe and let Madhav in. The latter immediately began exploring the whole dwelling in a hurry. It did not take long, since it was not a very large space. It was as though he was looking for something which he could not find. He stood with a glazed look for a few seconds, but soon he darted about, again, restless and frantic. After some time he sat in the living room for a bit – breathless, staring at the mantelpiece.

He then got up suddenly and went back to the bedroom. He stared at the four-poster bed for a while, and then looked up above the mahogany wardrobe. He pulled a chair, stood on it and reached for the old weathered shoe-box in which Arvind had kept his most treasured possessions – the photos of his once-perfect and beautiful family. Arvind stood back, stunned and baffled, but let Madhav do whatever he was trying to.

Scrambling desperately through the box, Madhav found a photograph of Mehak, Anamika and Arvind together, and instantly burst out crying with a guttural howl. Tears flowed down his face, as he was overcome! Demitri and Arvind watched this occurrence, totally confounded by what they were witnessing. Both thought that this could not be happening. It was inexplicable and unreal!

Then Madhav got up and he wrapped his arms around Arvind's waist in a tight embrace and pointed to and tapped his fingers repeatedly on the photos of Anamika and Mehak.

"What? What is it, Madhav?" asked Arvind anxiously.

"I know them! I know them!" repeated Madhav. They sat him down and tried to soothe him. Demitri brought him some chocolate milk and coconut biscuits. It took a good few minutes before he was calm enough for them to question him further.

"Do you know who they are?"

He shook his head.

"Have you met them?"

"No ... I don't know."

"Have you any idea how you know them?"

He shook his head again. They decided to give him a break and suggested he go to bed. Madhav readily agreed. He quickly fell asleep as soon as his head hit the pillow; as children often do when they are emotionally exhausted. Demitri and Arvind went to the living room, and Arvind poured each a large glass of wine.

That evening they sat on the porch outside Demitri's cottage. There was minimal small talk. It was sharing the silence, the darkness and stillness of the tea leaves that hid in the vast darkness, with just the humming and trilling of insects. Both were introspective and thought about all that had elapsed in recent days. Each had his feelings to deal with along with mutual respect for the other's emotions. Though it is evident that Arvind had a much bigger cross to bear, what was a revelation was the shadow all this had cast on Demitri – he was now a different person. His emotional compass seemed to have shifted.

They thought it might be a good idea to let Father know

the following day that they had reached safely and also apprise him of the latest developments, Demitri made the call. Father was also quite amazed by what had occurred. They agreed that it was okay for Madhav to stay on with them for a few more days, or until he felt comfortable; then they would drop him back to Vagamon.

Over the next few days, Madhav seemed to settle down. Children have this uncanny ability to switch off quickly after unsettling events, as though nothing has occurred. He loved the outdoors and was constantly wandering amongst the tea bushes. The tea pickers got to see a new face, and he often initiated conversations with them. In a short span of a few days, he became quite friendly and known to most. There were a few children of his age who lived not too far from the cottage. They would meet and play marbles and hopscotch. It was a welcome break from the regimented timelines and austere life at the ashram. It was the first time he could mingle with children in this way, an essential experience for any child. His likeable and easy-going nature lent a new colour and flavour to both of them also. They did not bring up the episode of the photographs again, although it constantly swirled in Arvind's head.

Children fortunately also have an innate ability to forget easily. They also adapt quickly to their surroundings. Madhav was no different; he readily settled and his week in Munnar passed soon. The following week they were ready to return to Vagamon. He was altogether a different child on the return trip, full of *joie de vivre* and had turned into an unstoppable chatterbox.

Father Edoardo was waiting for them when they pulled up in front of the gates at Holymath. Madhav quickly ran towards him and wrapped him in a tight embrace. There was also an evident, albeit repressed, show of joy from Father. He deeply loved this little boy, and it was the first time that Madhav had left the ashram in ten years! They had tea and once again feasted on the monastery's delicious sweets.

Once Madhav had disappeared to meet up with the other monks, who had also missed him, Father regained a bit of solemnity and spoke, "Arvind and Demitri, I have had time to dwell upon the recent events, and I feel we need to explore this situation a bit further. Arvind, what do you think about returning to Mumbai and taking Madhav with you? I do understand that it is a delicate matter for you, and it may not be something you are either ready or prepared for. However, if we have to get more answers, we must expose Madhav to those aspects of you and your past life that did not happen in Munnar."

He continued, "Of course, I will need to approach this subject with Madhav because as much as we need to find some answers, we need to be careful not to disturb him in such a way that it leaves him traumatised.

"Would you like to think about this once you return to Munnar? Meanwhile, I will work on Madhav. I feel that if this plan comes to fruition and the trip achieves what I hope it may, then it may well give him and, dare I say, you, some closure and clarification. Otherwise, I feel that this will impact his development as an adult. I might be hoping against hope, but I firmly believe that the Lord above works in mysterious ways, and as yet, we cannot even comprehend a drop of His Grace."

After spending a couple of hours, Arvind and Demitri said their goodbyes and climbed into the bug. Arvind braced himself for another assault on his spine from the rough ride ahead. Madhav was quite matter of fact with his goodbyes, although there was a fleeting glint of sadness visible in his eyes. No mention of a proposed trip to Mumbai was made at that point. Father said he would communicate with them over the next few days.

The drive back to Munnar seemed longer without Madhav; even in this short span, he had endeared himself to both of them. Demitri was not his cheery self: the change in his countenance ever since their first visit to Vagamon persisted. Arvind did not make an issue of it. They sat that evening on his porch, and for the first time, Demitri announced he would rather have coffee than tea or wine! He mumbled something about not being in the mood for alcohol. Arvind looked at him with raised eyebrows.

Over the next few weeks, they fell back into their routine. However, as they were like two retirees, there was plenty of time for contemplation. They were both deeply perplexed by the extraordinary coincidence of Madhav's and Mehak's timelines. Besides, Arvind could not get out of his mind the fact that Anamika bore twins, and the disappearance of one embryo, with no plausible medical explanation, had constantly and secretly bothered him. However, he had never let his wife know about his misgivings. Could it be a peculiar supernormal phenomenon? Was Madhav the lost twin? Re-embodiment? Impossible, he thought, but then how else could you explain all of this? He realised he did not know enough. He needed more information, knowledge and insight. He decided to go to Kochi to visit the Ernakulam Public Library, the oldest and one of the most extensive libraries in Kerala. Established in 1870, it houses an impressive range and collection of books suitable for both children as well as serious researchers.

He spent hours in the library over the next two days, poring over research articles about identical twins, reincarnation and afterlife, paranormal phenomenon – anything which he felt might give him some insight into all that had occurred. He found at least seventeen articles on the supernatural connection between twins. One recurrent theme was telepathy.

In one article, there was a report that a grandmother, who was an identical twin, had moved to Australia from England, while her twin stayed back. One day, she had an awful pain in one of her arms and couldn't explain it. She went to the hospital, but the doctors couldn't find anything wrong with the arm at all. About a week later, she received a letter from her twin, saying she had fallen and broken an arm – the same one in which the grandmother felt the pain, at that very time. There were numerous documented instances of premonition amongst twins when the other was in trouble or anguish. But nothing close to the supernatural as to what had surfaced with Madhav.

He found another documented story about twin sisters, where one twin narrated, 'I was taking a night class, and I suddenly got sick to my stomach and had an urge to call my sister immediately. I walked out of class and phoned her. She answered, but only to say she'd call me back. I walked back into the class, visibly shaken. My professor asked me if I was alright. I said, "No, I think my sister has been in a car accident..." My sister called me back ten minutes later. I had called her seconds after a car crashed into her!' There were many incidents of similar experiential nature.

There was also the other side of the coin. Some research concluded that there just isn't any conclusive proof at this point that twins have extra sensory perception or that twin telepathy exists.

In her book, 'Twin Mythconceptions', Dr. Nancy Segal, a pre-eminent twin researcher, states that anecdotes about twin telepathy reflect the loving, caring bond between the two. In those cases where twins were raised separately, but wore similar clothes and had matching tastes when they did meet, it reflects the genetic component of personality and interests. Segal adds that she does concede that if future studies ever show more concrete evidence of twin telepathy, she would be willing to re-examine her conclusions. However, there are many dimensions of twin behaviour that have no scientific explanations.

Arvind returned to Munnar, still perplexed and with no clarity on the issues at hand, especially of twins where one perished during pregnancy. Arvind also took some time and looked back over his life. Much of what had occurred seemed so surreal that he did not know what to, and what not to, believe. He thought it would be best to go with the flow of things and not overthink the matter.

He and Demitri had many intense debates about what was happening. He was impressed by the depth and breadth of his neighbour's knowledge. He had rarely had a chance to explore this facet of his friend's personality, and newfound respect resulted from all of this.

They both agreed it was *purgatorio*.

It was the better part of five weeks before they finally heard from Father Edoardo. He had spoken to Madhav a few weeks after his return, and this amicable child had readily accepted whatever Father had suggested, and was willing to travel as and when he was asked to. By now Arvind had reconciled to the fact that retuning to Mumbai was necessary.

With that affirmation, they started to make travel plans. Initially, Demitri was a bit reluctant to make the trip. There was too much inertia from his comfortable existence in Munnar and was unwilling to leave his nest for a prolonged period. For him, Mumbai might as well have been Mars! On the other hand, there was also a bit of intrigue and a quest to find an answer to this increasingly baffling puzzle.

The final travel plan was to go down to Kochi and take a flight to Pune. From Pune, they would travel to Mumbai by road. This would give Madhav a chance to pass through the same route that was the final journey of Anamika and Mehak, except that it would be from the opposite direction. Father suggested this and raised it gingerly with Arvind. Initially, Arvind refused as he did not feel he could pass through that baptism of fire again, and his heart could not take the pain of revisiting that spot where the ravine had swallowed his family.

But Father had a great gift of making the impossible possible. He convinced Arvind that it was vital that Madhav passed through that precise spot. He stated that the fall would have been the moment of most tremendous emotional upheaval and distress for both mother and daughter before they met their maker so mercilessly. If there is anything lingering in the ether or some telepathic communion, it would be at the spot of maximum anguish and turmoil. If there is any truth that a twin can share such intense, painful moments, then it would be that very place that Madhav would perceive more than any other. Difficult as it may be, it may well contribute more insight into the whole situation.

Arvind reluctantly conceded to Father's greater wisdom.

□

15

Memories have more colours than a rainbow. Not merely a sunset orange, a blood-red or a sky blue – there is black and white, and there is grey. Memories also have lifetimes tucked into their pocket, centuries hemmed into their lining with the music of love, songs of angst, troves of laughter, fables, triumph and tragedy woven into their fabric. The rain cannot wash, nor can the wind blow them away. They live not only in our subconscious minds but in the deeper crevices of our very being. We are barely aware of them as the present drowns them into the deep waters of our past.

The mere thought of returning to Mumbai was scorching Arvind's soul with cinders from the past. Those which never fully extinguish just smoulder softly within, until your last breath. He was profoundly disturbed and restless inside, though it was not evident on the surface. He decided he would harness every ounce of courage and grit that he could, bite the bullet and make the journey.

They drove down to Kochi, cramped in the rustic Beetle with a large volume of luggage and accessories. Arvind was now getting accustomed to Demitri's style of travel and driving. It took a long time to convince him that it would not be cold in Mumbai. They boarded a flight from Kochi airport and within two hours, touched down in Pune. It is an exhilarating experience for any child boarding an aeroplane for the first time, and Madhav was no exception. He remained glued to the aeroplane window and took it all in – the spectacular experience that a first flight is. The roar of the 737, heard for the first time, is felt in the pit of the stomach as the plane climbs. How the world below turns smaller and smaller till nothing is discernible! The passing in and out of the fluffy clouds and the dazzling sunshine skimming off the wings, the endless sky and the diminishing earth and the world below that you leave beneath lend a new perspective in size. He was entranced by it all. There was a gleam of marvel in his young eyes.

Pune was an entirely different city from what Madhav was accustomed to. The novelty of the experience was evident in his reactions and expressions. They stayed over for a day. The following morning, they bundled into a rental car, a Toyota – far more spacious than the Beetle, much to the relief of Madhav and Arvind.

Arvind felt his discomfiture building up right from the outset. The Mumbai-Pune Expressway was India's first six-lane concrete, high-speed, access controlled, tolled expressway. It spans a distance of 94.5 kms connecting Mumbai, the capital of the state of Maharashtra and the financial capital of India, with Pune, the cultural capital of Maharashtra and an industrial and educational hub. It is a picturesque drive for anyone, as it cuts through the heart of the Western Ghats mountain range. However, Arvind knew it would be a big challenge to get through this stretch of tarmac. It would be the second longest drive of his life, and he was unsure what toll it would take on him. At that point, he was not so concerned about how Madhav would respond because the boy had no way of knowing what lay before him. He had no known strings attached.

Arvind reminisced about his beautiful wife and his short but joyful marriage, his perfect life. The words of a W.B. Yeats' couplet came to him:

"How far away the stars seem, and how far is our first kiss, and ah, how old my heart! Ephemera."

Madhav sat at the edge of his seat, bright-eyed and with

pupils as dilated as can be. He took in the scenery whizzing past in delightful gulps, as he had never been on such a highway and in a vehicle that travelled so fast. He had but a few times sat in an automobile that had gently made its way around the slow track around Vagamon. His previous longest journey was from Vagamon to Kochi in a lazy Beetle. He particularly loved the tunnels, and there were six of these. He got overexcited and clapped his hands vigorously through the tunnels. He was talking excitedly to Demitri and Arvind. He found it fascinating how it turned dark and light again; children find the most ordinary things magical! He did not enjoy the occasional downpour that they met as he was so used to rain.

As they crept closer to the fateful site well before the Khandala tunnel, Arvind started to feel a sense of deep uneasiness. He did not know how he would cope when they reached the spot. Even in all his frenzy during that fateful day, he still vividly remembered the precise location of the accident. It was a memory etched in torment. He recalled a verse that his mother used to recite in her daily prayers;

"Jehi vidhi hoi Nath
Hit moora
Karahu so vegi dass
Main tor."

'O Lord, I know not where I am headed or what lies ahead of me, nor what direction to take. I surrender to thee to do whatever thou deemest best for me.'

Once they entered the Khandala tunnel, there was a noticeable change in Madhav's demeanour. To start with, he became very still and silent (the accident had occurred before entering the tunnel on the Mumbai side). Though Arvind immediately noted this, he did not show any reaction. As soon as they came out of the other end and their car was met by cascading sunlight coming from behind the hills, Madhav started trembling. As the vehicle approached the actual site of the crash, about which he could have no clue as Arvind had never mentioned anything to him, he started to wail –

smacking his lips intermittently. Then slowly his body started contorting, progressing to severe spasms. He placed his hands over his ears, drew his knees up to his chest, wrapped his arms in front of his shins, started rocking his body back and forth, and screamed at the top of his voice, "Stop the car! Stop the car!!"

Although vehicles are not allowed to stop on the highway, the driver they had hired with the car was so astounded by the screaming that he instinctively jammed the brakes and stopped in the slow lane. Madhav opened his car door and jumped out in a flash. He ran towards the edge of the expressway right at the tunnel's exit, where it had been cut through the heart of the mountain. He screamed incessantly and pointed to the ravine below, shouting: "There! There!!!" His outstretched arm and finger were pointing to the bottom at the exact spot from where they had pulled up the mangled remains of the car with Arvind's lost family inside. A few tiny broken pieces of the tail-lights remained scattered at the edge of the road, even now.

Arvind had caught up with him by this time, and he immediately wrapped his arms around Madhav from behind to make sure he did not leap or go over the edge in his frenzy. However, Madhav was quite difficult to control as though he had superhuman strength and fought violently with every ounce of his being for Arvind to let him go, but Arvind held on. By this time, Demitri and the driver had caught up with them, and together they reined in this upset and disturbed child and brought him back to safety from the edge of the expressway. By this time, many other passing vehicles had seen the commotion and were intrigued. They slowed, some stopped, and a few pulled over; some honked their horns in annoyance as they went by, others let out streams of profanity before moving on, while most others ignored the commotion and kept on driving.

Over the next few minutes, they managed to calm him down quite a bit and got him back in the car. He was still sobbing uncontrollably. By this time, the gravity of what had just happened had dawned upon Arvind and Demitri. Arvind did not get a chance to reconcile or even acknowledge his feelings as Madhav's reaction had been so overwhelming.

They spent some more time in pacifying the boy. After he was a bit more settled, they asked what had happened.

He replied, "I don't know, but ... but ... Mehak?"

He knew the names – Anamika and Mehak since he had seen their photographs at the cottage in Munnar. This one statement was enough for both of them to understand that there could not be a surer sign that there was a connection between him and Mehak!

Was he the 'lost twin', if any such thing were possible? They had no scientific explanation, but what was taking place before their very own eyes could not be denied.

They decided to take a break at the next road-side services before entering Mumbai. Once back on the road, they drove the rest of the journey in silence. Demitri held the quivering child's hand for the remainder of the trip. Arvind knew that Anamika's parents had a house on the outskirts of Mumbai, which was approaching fast. He decided not to stop there as he thought they might not be very pleased to see him, after his sudden disappearance from the face of the earth two years ago. He knew that they too would have searched high and low for him. He had not communicated with them or his parents. Even they did not know whether he was dead or alive. He gave directions to the driver, who drove them to their apartment block just off Pedder Road. His parents lived on the sixth floor.

Demitri had insisted that they book a hotel room, but Arvind had convinced Demitri that they should try his parents' house first. He knew if he were to return to Mumbai, he would need to correct the many wrongs he had done by his sudden disappearance. It was going to be a profoundly challenging tryst for Arvind – to face his parents. But it would still be little compared to what they would have been through. What could he possibly say to them that would make up for or atone or justify the pain and anguish that he had caused them by leaving suddenly, especially as they were also still reeling under the shock of losing Anamika and Mehak? He had abandoned them. It was a triple tragedy for them. He never made a single call to them – no word, nor a call. Even though it was his way of coping and surviving the ordeal, it did not validate the untold misery he had put them through. He had no idea how they would react. He knew that they would have been traumatised deeply, and when there was no communication from him for a few months, would have assumed the worst.

It scorched his soul with guilt to consider what he had done. But due to the tragic chain of events, he had walked away in a fog of abject hopelessness. Once in Munnar, he felt that all connection with his past needed to be severed for him to remain barely alive and keep his sanity. Somehow, he had shelved their existence and their pain in another heart. He could not survive with any reminder of his past life. He realised that it was selfish and cruel to them, but that was the way he had learned to exist. Had it not been for Madhav, this day of homecoming would probably never have come.

He felt remorseful and hesitant now, trembling inside with regret, guilt and apprehension as he stood outside the door of their flat with Demitri and Madhav in tow. Demitri placed a supporting hand on his shoulder, and Madhav held and squeezed his hand and smiled as though he too understood.

The time was about half past one in the afternoon, and if he remembered correctly, his father always ate his lunch at one. He was disciplined and meticulous about his mealtimes. Arvind decided not to ring the doorbell. Instead, he braced himself, drew a long and deep breath and knocked on the door softly.

A 'bai' (housemaid) opened the door. Arvind did not recognize her. She was new; perhaps, the old one had left. She too had no idea who he was.

"Who do you want?" she asked curtly.

"Who is it?" he heard his father's baritone voice coming from his study.

"I don't know, sahib," she responded.

By this time Arvind's father had come to the door. As he looked up to question what the visitor wanted, he met the eyes of his only son. Resilient though he was, his legs just buckled, and shouted for his wife as he fell to the floor. She came hurrying, worried something had happened. When she laid eyes upon Arvind, she too slumped to the floor in a heap next to him. They both came around quickly and thankfully, unhurt. Once his parents had somewhat regained their composure, they all embraced and wept together. Arvind's father invited Demitri and Madhav in.

Arvind apologised profusely. No matter what he had put them through, after an initial chiding to their son, expressing their deep annoyance and the trauma and heartbreak that they had endured, his parents readily forgave him – so immense was their joy that their son was well and alive. It was nothing short of a miracle for them. It was as though Deepavali (the Festival of Lights) had come early. Their joy was boundless!

Arvind introduced Demitri. It took another couple of hours for Arvind to bring them up to date with the last two years, and explain how Madhav was the reason for his return.

Arvind's mother got up, kissed and embraced Madhav.

□

16

The next few days were a whirlwind of family and friends' reunion and the therapy of parental pampering. A lot of people were upset, friends furious but forgiving, some overjoyed. Surprisingly, as the information spread, Arvind was moved by the number of his old patients who had turned up at the doorstep of his parents' flat. His legacy had not been forgotten. Indeed, all the excellent work that he had done was evident in their words and gratitude.

Demitri spent his days exploring Mumbai – he was taken by the sights and sounds, and bewildered by how everything worked amid so much chaos! He was, however, too scared to jump on to a Mumbai local train; he preferred the friendly BEST buses.

Arvind felt relieved somehow. However, the absence of his wife and daughter was also a painful aide-memoire of the past, and at times he felt this overwhelming emotion to get up and walk away again. Every street corner, every sight and sound were a cruel reminder, and his wounds were constantly re-opened. It was the very thing he feared and it had made him run away. His heart pined for them.

While all this was going on, Madhav was being treated like a lost grandchild by Arvind's parents, and his company was like a poultice for them. He was spoilt down to the tee and treated like royalty. Arvind's parents passed the news of his homecoming to his in-laws, and they decided to come down from Pune in the next few days. When they arrived, his profuse apologies to them were readily accepted. After all, he was the only part of their daughter's family that was still alive.

A few days later, amongst the many visitors was the Member of Parliament, Pramod Sinha, a family friend. He made a big show of how much he had missed Arvind and how sorry he felt about his loss. He emphasised it repeatedly, to such an extent that it felt like an overkill and reeked of insincerity and pretence! While he was still with them, sipping tea and munching homemade *samosas*, Madhav returned from playing cricket with other kids in the parking lot of the building.

Arvind introduced him, "Madhav, this is Mr. Sinha; he is a politician." Madhav looked at him but did not say anything.

Arvind asked, "What's the matter, Madhav?"

"Nothing," responded Madhav quite slowly. With that, he turned and left the room. Arvind was surprised but did not make any bones about it. Once Pramod Sinha had left, he quizzed Madhav, "What happened when you met that gentleman?"

All he got back was, "I don't know."

A few days passed, and one evening the doorbell rang. Arvind's mom called out to Madhav, "Can you please get that, Madhav?"

It was Mr Sinha's chauffeur, and he said that his boss had sent some gifts for the family. But he needed a hand to bring them up to the apartment. Madhav readily offered, and once Arvind's mother gave him the nod, he went down six floors with the man. There was a black, 7-series BMW parked at the rear end of the parking lot. They went straight to the boot. Madhav had picked some stuff to carry, and as he turned, he caught a glimpse of someone sitting in the passenger seat of the BMW – he screamed and dropped his load. His scream was so loud that it was heard through the open balcony windows on the sixth floor!

Arvind shouted from the balcony, "O God, what now?"

He ran down the six flights of stairs and found Madhav standing there, trembling and pale.

"What happened, son?" he asked.

A shaking of the head was all he got. Arvind asked the chauffeur to leave and took the boy back to the flat.

Once he had settled, Arvind asked him again, "What's the matter?"

"It was that man in the car!"

Since Arvind knew him as Ram Singh, who was Mr. Sinha's trusted aide, right-hand man-cum-Man Friday, and personal bodyguard, Arvind was surprised, "What about him?"

"I don't exactly know, but something about him is familiar," replied Madhav.

"That's impossible!" said Arvind.

But then he drew in a sharp breath. Madhav's premonitions had so far proved right. But what could be the connection?

They left that issue at that.

Quite some time had now passed since they had all been in Mumbai, and the initial excitement and social visits had reduced. The inevitable conversation of 'what next?' was cropping up. In the meantime, Demitri had had his bellyful of the big city and longed to go back to the land of tea leaves. He had decided not to consume any alcohol till he got back, and possibly, his sobriety and pledge were getting the better of him. Arvind went to visit his former clinic one day. Some of his staff already knew that he was back; others were pleasantly surprised. They told him that the patients missed him greatly, and many had never gotten over his leaving.

The clinic, of course, had been sold in haste, and a new doctor was appointed immediately. This time, however, it was led by Dr. Pradeep Sharma. He was from Saharanpur in the state of Uttar Pradesh, and seemingly had never even visited Mumbai before.

Arvind was told in confidence by his senior staff, who still worked there, that both the clientele and workings of the clinic had sadly changed. There seemed to be a lot of concerned patients, as many activities unrelated to the practice of medicine were going on. The clinic would sometimes be open till midnight, which was strange, considering that there were no patients at that hour. The patients were being managed quite poorly, and the staff was treated indifferently. Many of the old-timers had already resigned and left. Many long-standing patients were now defecting to other clinics in the area.

Arvind felt a pang of regret. All the goodwill and trust that he had sowed had been lost by one decisive stroke of destiny. He began feeling more confident that there was no place for him in this city. The question was how to deal with his parental situation, and what was to happen to Madhav. He had been in regular touch with Father Edoardo and kept him updated. Father was in no desperate hurry to have him back, mainly as Madhav had conveyed that he was happy and enjoying himself. However, he had told Arvind that they needed to make a firm and early decision about where the child's future lay.

Madhav and Arvind started to get along rather well, and a robust relationship was forged. He was beginning to enjoy a somewhat paternal role. As he had much more time on his hands than he had with Mehak, he could partake in many activities that the boy wanted. But he was well aware that Madhav's future direction needed to be decided and that too, soon. He was also concerned about the increasingly vital 'surrogate' grandparent and grandchild bond that was rapidly developing.

Arvind had always been a walker. He invariably spent endless hours every day in Munnar just walking, often with no planned route. It was his outlet, his catharsis, his haven. It had been his saviour, his redemption and his salvation.

Walking amid those green shrubs and hills had helped him connect with nature and had freed his soul from some of his sorrow and guilt. It was the reason why he had survived his ordeal.

He decided to resume his activity and started going out for long walks; sometimes Madhav would accompany him.

Mostly he walked alone.

□

17

On one such long walk, Arvind, lost deep in his thoughts, had drifted off his usual route. He found himself in a neglected and isolated small city park. It wasn't used much as it was adjacent to a neglected cemetery, and most people felt a bit jittery coming there. He stepped into the cemetery, walked about observing the varied gravestones and wondered what life is and the 'much ado about nothing'. He was so lost in a deep, dark cloud of thoughts that he lost track of both time and place. He paused to get his bearings. The evening was drawing in and darkness seemed to have set in swiftly. It was soon pitch black. The moonless sky looked amorphous. He sat on a knee-high stone next to an unnamed grave surrounded by overgrown weeds and tall grass, for some rest and to gather himself. He was about to get up and return home when he heard some rustling behind him. As he turned sharply, a short, thin silhouette emerged from the shrubbery.

"Doctor *sahib,*" the man said in a hushed whisper. He spoke in rustic, rural Marathi (the language spoken in Maharashtra state) dialect. "*Namaste*!" he bowed as he spoke and stayed in that posture for a long time.

Arvind was caught unawares and, for a second, he almost jumped out of his skin. As he regained his composure, he asked, "Who are you?" as he took a couple of steps backwards.

"Doctor *sahib*, I am Rawat. You might remember me. I

used to work for Mr. Pramod Sinha." Having spoken, he moved into the light streaming from a street lamp, which allowed Arvind to identify him. Even though he looked impoverished and wasted, he was who he said he was and still easily recognisable. Arvind relaxed a bit.

"Why are you hiding in this manner?" he asked curtly, as the man had emerged the shadows like someone who wanted to ambush him.

"Doctor *sahib*, it's because I cannot run the risk of being seen talking to you. That is why I had to wait for such a long time and a place such as this. I have been shadowing you for days but have never got an opportunity to speak to you covertly till today."

Arvind was a bit suspicious but intrigued at the same time.

"Okay," he relented.

"Doctor *sahib*, please step a bit nearer the trees and into the dark area. I promise that there is no reason to fear me, I assure you," he whispered with folded hands.

Arvind was in a situation that he felt he had very little to lose. He moved into the cover of the trees, shielded from the direct light of the streetlamp. "Go ahead."

Rawat immediately fell at Arvind's feet, "Doctor *sahib*, first of all, I have come to seek your forgiveness."

"For what?"

"For what I am about to tell you."

"Okay."

"I know who killed your wife and daughter."

"What!" exclaimed Arvind at the top of his voice.

"Ssshh, please *sahib*," pleaded Rawat. "Please hear me out."

Arvind nodded in stunned silence. The man stood up slowly.

"Sir, when the accident happened, I was working for Mr. Sinha, as you might remember. I have also been to your house with him, even at times while you were at your clinic. Now and again, Mr. Sinha would visit your home in the middle of the day. Don't misunderstand, your wife was always very decent and dignified, but we, that is, all those in the close circles of Mr. Sinha knew that he had his evil eye on her; he made no secret of it. He was extremely envious of you, and often expressed openly that he wished he could get rid of you. But he knew that to try and harm you directly would be a step too far, and he did not want that. So he decided to do it in a more sly and devious manner. As you are aware, all these extortion gangs work in cahoots with corrupt politicians, and the favours run both ways. He decided to set one of these gangs on you. Their job was to systematically destroy your career and medical practice by intimidation, threats and extortion and drive you to the ground in the process. He carefully planned to destroy you professionally, financially and psychologically, eventually forcing you to give up your practice and thereby break-up your personal and marital life and compel you to do something drastic or illegal. He would then have you out of his way one way or other, without any trace of his being directly involved. Sorry, but he had his 'eyes on the prize'."

Arvind felt an intense surge of anger and disbelief rise within his chest and a constriction in his throat. The man paused and licked his cracked and parched lips and continued, "He, however, got very impatient and restless. He was so obsessed with your wife that he decided to up the ante and hatched a plan to terrorise you by intimidating your family in a big way – something so drastic that would deeply hurt and upset you.

"He knew that you were going to send your wife and daughter away early morning on that fateful day. He sent a truck with a couple of his henchmen after them, and the idea was to nudge the car's rear spoiler, cause a minor mishap, a small accident, just enough to put the fear of God in them and wound you further. I was not there as he had sent me to purchase some drugs down in Koregaon. But I know what happened as I have it from the horse's mouth, the driver.

"Who was the driver?" butted in Arvind.

"It was Ram Singh, *sahib*."

"Oh, my dear God!" He realised that this might explain Madhav's outburst the other day when he saw Ram Singh sitting in the car – something inside that child knew who it was.

"Okay, go on."

"What happened on that day was not exactly what was planned. It started raining quite heavily, and the visibility was poor. Unexpectedly, as the truck was closing in on your wife's car, another car rapidly overtook it. This forced the driver to slow down, so what was intended to be a minor bumper to bumper shove ended up being a stronger collision. By now, there was water on the road. Your wife's car skidded, hydroplaned, spun and went over the verge at the edge of the cliff, ending up in the ravine."

Arvind slid down on the grass and buried his face in his hands, and sobbed uncontrollably. It was as though someone had trampled on his heart and then set it on fire. He was in *Dante's inferno*.

Rawat simply stood there in silence with his hands folded and head bowed in shame, tearful and whimpering. Finally, Arvind regained some composure to ask, "Why did you not try and expose this plan before the event?"

"Doctor *sahib*, there were three reasons: firstly, I was a loyal servant and second, nobody dares to cross a man like Mr Sinha. He is a devious and dangerous man. Also, the accident was never meant to end fatally; the main aim was merely to scare your family."

"Why are you telling me this now?" There was anger in his tone.

"*Sahib*, it is because he has crossed the line with my family too. Soon after this event, my wife came to Mumbai for the first time since we wed about three years earlier. I was away on another one of his drug drop-offs in Bangalore when she arrived. She is a lovely maiden from the hills of Himachal

Pradesh. On the first day she landed, he forced himself on her and strong-armed her to have sex with him. An innocent village girl, overawed, could not fend him off. In fact, for many days she was unable to tell me. After that, she completely lost her bearing, her life was shattered, her being disrupted, and she was under psychiatric treatment for a long time. Her condition did not settle and she is now back home in our village, but it has wrecked her soul and almost destroyed our marriage.

I left his employment immediately despite death threats. There were a few physical attacks on me, and these broke a few bones. It was then I had decided that I would tell you everything, but you had disappeared. Nobody knew where you were, so I could not find you. It is only now since I came to know of your return that I have been tailing you."

Arvind was shocked and devastated. He could not believe what he had just heard: Pramod Sinha – a man he considered a true and trusted family friend! He could never have fathomed that he was a person of such evil disposition. It was as though a lava of disgust and rage engulfed him. They both sat for a little while in silence. Then Rawat asked for permission to speak, "May I say something, *sahib*?"

"Yes."

"I know that you are rightly enraged and I cannot even try to comprehend what you are feeling right now, and would like him punished for this terrible crime. But he is a widely connected man with strong political influence and tentacles extending to the mafia and the underworld. You cannot take him on as you would an average criminal. He is well beyond the reach of the police and the law; he carries them both in his back pocket.

"You will have to adopt a carefully planned strategy; a bullish approach is sure to fail. He will ruthlessly eliminate you."

He folded his hands and once again fell at Arvind's feet and begged his forgiveness. He handed Arvind his telephone number. "Doctor *sahib*, if there is anything I can do to help you and in some way atone for my sins, please call me, day or night."

With that, he turned and vanished into the dark like a ghost. Arvind stood there for a second, wondering if it was real or a delusion.

He walked back home numb, in an unconscious daze.

□

18

The Member of Parliament was all of six feet two, suave and clean-shaven. He had a crop of dense, black, stubborn, curly hair that was always trimmed to perfection. Bestowed with good looks, he had a semblance of Kashmiri political royalty. He looked like a male version of the late Indira Gandhi. He had a strong athletic body and was always immaculately dressed. He was innately brilliant with an IQ falling into the genius category. Ever since his childhood, he had the gift of switching his personality into different modes effortlessly. He could be soft, gentle and compassionate; or vicious and violent! He could be a picture of diplomacy, nifty as a fox or brutally blunt. As he turned into an adolescent, he became vain, astute, conniving and sly. He was also strong-headed, steadfast and fearless. He was a grandmaster at human manipulation. With natural ease, he played his siblings, parents, friends, and anyone with whom he came into contact without them realising they were being used against each other. He excelled at his studies though was contemptuous of his teachers and the education system. He was a brilliant sportsman and quickly rose to the pedestal of a Head Boy by his final year at school – an actual Machiavellian prince in the making!

He grew into a strong-willed, cold, calculating and an unscrupulous young man who wanted it all. He had disregard for anything or anyone who stood in his way. People who are willing to pay any price for what they want often end up getting it.

He started his political career at the young age of fifteen when he befriended a member of the Youngmen's Congress and immediately enrolled. He was not interested in any partisan politics; he just wanted the power and the fame. It became evident to him that politics was the quickest way to attain both unbridled power and wealth. He began as a minor peddler once he understood the demand and importance of high-quality alcohol in these circles. He became a covert bootlegger. He quickly graduated to supplying recreational drugs and women when he realised how dependent the politicians were upon these. It was easy for him to do this as he was just a kid. He was caught a couple of times but got away after he apologised profusely and begged forgiveness – he was considered just a misguided teenager. He was quickly getting better at this business with every passing day and was beginning to cover his tracks well. He started to keep a secret diary of all the politicians and whom they slept with, along with their drugs needs and bad habits, what and how much he had supplied, with dates and times.

With passing years, he polished his skills and sharpened his Machiavellian nails. He understood the dirty game called politics right down to its roots and honed it into a fine art. It helps if you start young. It also helps if you are willing to sacrifice anything and you are wicked to the core. He had also collected a few favours for being discreet and saved a good deal of money in the process.

He soon started organising political demonstrations, movements and social disruptions for the senior politicians against the opposition. He was able to do these discreetly and effectively; he deputised shrewdly. Soon enough, he started to get noticed in the higher corridors of power. In politics, unfortunately, it is the scum that often rises to the top.

His first break came when he was awarded the presidency of the Youth Ajanta political party. This appointment immediately brought him to the table with the big boys. All politicians want to harness power and vote bank of the youth, especially in India, where they hold such a large chunk of it, given their numbers. Even the seasoned politicians, crooked as they were, did not realise that they were dealing with an altogether different kettle of fish. He had a level of foresight, tenacity, ferocity and guile that is rare even amongst their degenerate breed.

He seemed destined to rise. He quickly moved up the ranks and was soon rubbing shoulders with Members of Parliament and cabinet ministers. He was often present at the Rashtrapati Bhavan, mingling with the who's who of Indian politics and all this by the time he turned twenty-one!

His ambitions were soaring, and he now began gathering intimate knowledge of every dirty pie, every kickback and the underhand dealings of his peers. He was not afraid to confront, manipulate and even gently intimidate them. Gifted with good looks and a silver tongue, he was often in with their wives and daughters, many of whom fell for him as he behaved like a perfect gentleman while harbouring the darkest thoughts. They never had the faintest clue about his intentions. Many succumbed to his charms, but he always made sure he had enough on them to blackmail them if they were to consider breaking their silence. He gathered and held incriminating evidence; so had them exactly where he wanted.

Slowly but surely, he developed his power bank, his coterie of thugs, loyal young politicians, policemen, drug-peddlers, pimps, slum dwellers, and good-for-nothing stragglers. He also had some do-gooders and social workers on his tab. You name it, the potpourri was complex. He cultivated people from all walks of life and all professions. He was in it for the long run; he understood a career in politics is a marathon, and never considered it a sprint. His blueprint for political success had an almost flawless design.

Within years he became a name to reckon with amongst the political circles. Everyone wanted to be on his right side. As his political graph rose, simultaneously unbeknownst, except to his closest, his underworld network and murky business empire also blossomed. He nurtured close links with the mafia, gang lords, con-men, hitmen, Dubai underworld bosses, and wheeler-dealers of all sorts. Initially, he had small shares and stakes in the criminal underbelly of Mumbai, but slowly and surely he acquired more interest and took control of many such dens. Over time, he diversified his dirty empire into drugs, prostitution and gambling. Gold-smuggling, *hawala*, kidnapping and extortion were also thrown in the mix.

However, what was different about him compared to your average corrupt politician was that he had kept his hands and image clean, and covered his tracks meticulously. No phone calls or SIM cards could be traced back to him; there was never any written trace, and his accounts seemed squeaky clean. He never kept any black money close to him. It was all laundered and deposited in the helpful banks of small and accommodating countries in Europe, such as Liechtenstein and Luxembourg. It was almost impossible to find any footprints or trails that led back to him.

He was amassing a fortune. With all his attributes, he was quite naturally a womaniser. He was purely interested in sexual relationships, so it did not matter who it was with. Since he was never emotionally invested, he did not care but was careful not to upset the powers that be, and if it did come to that at times, he always held all the right cards! Also, he had kept a catalogue of photographs, videos and many hidden 'dirty little secrets' of all the women he had serviced. He always held leverage.

It was not long, and as expected that by the age of thirty-two, he became a Member of Parliament. Even though it seemed a bit late for someone of his potential, he had grown deep roots. He had finally stepped into big political shoes.

The rise of Pramod Sinha had just begun!

□

19

Arvind was profoundly distressed and very contemplative for the next few days and suffered tormented and sleepless nights. He understood that Rawat had given him sound advice about not reacting or being obvious to Pramod Sinha. But could he believe Rawat's story? Why would he say all this? What was his credibility? Did the dots join up when he tried to analyse? Somehow, they did! What seemed to come across was utter honesty and sincerity, along with remorse in the man's narration of how things had come to pass.

But what next?

To attempt and incriminate a man of Pramod Sinha's stature would be no mean feat. It could only be approached using an 'out of the box' and lateral-thinking approach. The man considered himself above the law. Thus, the question was how to go about it?

After much deliberation, he thought it would be worth taking advice once again from his old friend Krishan, who he remembered was working at RAW when they last spoke. It was one of the few autonomous bodies different from usually corrupt government institutions widely prevalent in India. He decided to make the call, and he was lucky that Krishan was still there. He was now the number two man at RAW and tipped to become the head of RAW within the following year. He was gracious and happy to hear from Arvind once again.

"Hello Arvind, good to hear from you. I am truly sorry to hear about your wife and daughter. It was in the news, so I got to know. I tried to call you a couple of times, but your number was unreachable."

"Yes, I am sorry too. It was soul-destroying, and I just walked away from it all, but certain recent events have brought me back to Mumbai. Since I have returned, there have been a lot of developments. I wondered if I could come down to Delhi and speak to you face to face; telephones are impersonal and not secure. I would like to see you anyway."

"Sure, that would be great. Why don't you come this weekend? I have some time off, and you can stay with me."

"Fine," agreed Arvind.

That Friday, Arvind boarded the early morning flight from Mumbai to Delhi. Krishan had sent an official vehicle and a couple of his flunkies to receive him. Krishan met him with a warm embrace. The RAW man once again was very sympathetic and truly sad at what had elapsed.

Arvind narrated the detailed passage of events, including Madhav's unique perceptions and Rawat's versions of the incident.

"I can't let him go scot-free, Krishan," said Arvind. He was feeling a surge of uncontrollable rage and emotions rise within him.

"No, I agree. I am fortunately in a much stronger position now and have a lot more control over how I may help you. Is Rawat willing to be a witness?"

"I am afraid not; he is petrified at the thought of any backlash from Pramod to his extended family. But he will be happy to work as an informer. He has a lot of insider knowledge of Pramod's illicit operations."

"Well, we will just have to find another way around it." With that, Krishan picked up the phone and spoke to five different people within ten minutes. His authority and the power of his chair was evident.

"Arvind, please be aware that this man is extremely

dangerous. I would advise that you must never show even a glimmer of altered behaviour whenever you meet him. He must never be able to suspect that you might be stirring up things behind the scene."

The phone rang. Krishan listened quite intently. He then turned to Arvind and spoke, "We have had a bit of luck: we already have a RAW file on him, and apparently, he also has some hand in arms dealing, which has placed him within our ambit. This matter enables me to make it official and easy for me to escalate a dispatch on him. Unknown to the majority of countries, we have some of the most advanced surveillance software on the planet. Some of our programmes have been borrowed and are being used by the CIA. We shall have him fully tapped in no time!"

"Thank you, Krishan. I am deeply grateful for your help," said Arvind.

"Not at all. On the contrary, our friend here is quite a major player, and his hands are also into black marketing, gambling, including online betting in cricket. He is also involved in organ trading. Such a person must be brought to justice. If we can see this through, you would have done us and your country a favour. The only caveat is that he is a politician, and they can be very slippery because the mud often splashes to the top."

Arvind nodded in agreement.

"Of course, I believe that his driver, Ram Singh or whatever his name is, will play a pivotal role. He will need to be roped in one way or another."

With that, he stood, stretched his hand towards Arvind, who met it with a firm, grateful double-handed handshake.

"Leave it with me," were his parting words.

□

20

Arvind was back in Mumbai within four hours of that conversation. He did not give a clear explanation or account to his parents about why he had gone to Delhi, and he just told them never to bring it up in front of anybody. They found his request somewhat mysterious but dutifully respected his wishes and held their silence.

Arvind met Pramod socially on a couple of occasions during the next few weeks, and he seemed to be a bit preoccupied. Arvind, however, managed to keep a neutral front. He was neither over-friendly nor indifferent. But he certainly got the feeling that something was stirring behind the scenes for Pramod.

A few days later, at about midnight, Arvind got a call from Krishan. An operation, called '*Lynx*', was well underway. RAW had touched base with Rawat, and he was cooperating fully. They were working on securing Ram Singh as an operative ('informer' in other terminology). They had a well-defined methodology. He told Arvind that Ram Singh was being offered a deal. If he agreed to become an operative and provide information that eventually led to a conviction against Pramod, he was likely to get off with a lighter suspended sentence of five years. Ram Singh was, however, greedy and bartering for an acquittal. That was unlikely to happen, given that he was likely to be charged with manslaughter.

Meanwhile, Madhav's educational needs were suffering during this time. Earlier, he was being schooled locally at the ashram, but this whole affair had disrupted that. Arvind decided to tutor him personally, but it was inadequate as he was preoccupied with other issues. After a long consideration, Arvind decided it might be in Madhav's best interest if he returned to Holymath ashram for now. They returned to Kochi by train this time. It was at Madhav's request. He had developed a fascination with all things 'railway' related. He would often travel on his own on the Mumbai local trains to and fro just for fun. His favourite route was the one that shuttled between Borivali and Churchgate. He even ventured during the peak rush hour now and again, just for the challenge. He got squashed and sandwiched between the milling numbers in the overcrowded trains, but he enjoyed that bit too. He had now spent nearly four months in Mumbai.

A cross-country train journey in India is like tasting a slice of the nation. India is more like a continent than a country, and a train journey is a microcosm. Madhav enjoyed the long trip and took it all in. It was gratifying for Arvind to be able to see that sparkle in this child's eyes, eyes that they held no veil of prejudice, no preconceived notions or cynicism, no race or rank, and no moral judgements. He was a clean canvas, not spoilt by age and all the layers with which adults are tainted. Arvind had lost all his spark on that one fateful day.

The folks at the ashram were delighted to have their little mascot, 'Son from Fortune' back. He was still a charming lad, full of smiles and eagerness, but they did notice a slight change in his aspect. There was an added air of sobriety about him. Father Edoardo was, of course, observant and well aware of what the child was going through. He was particularly concerned about Madhav's developmental and educational needs, and that these had been derailed for a short period. He did not know what the future might hold, but he wanted to ensure that the disruption was not detrimental or too prolonged. He had therefore encouraged Madhav's return to

Holymath. He was also acutely aware that it was happenstance that this child was raised amongst a brotherhood, but that did not mean that he should adopt this way of life as his chosen or destined path. If he were to choose such a road of his own volition, that would be fine. Any imposition, however, would be inappropriate.

He felt that exposure to other professions, vocations and ways of life was paramount for the lad. He wanted to avoid a situation where Madhav would be committed and trapped in a life that he was never meant for. Father was well aware that this commitment, although essential, had also been the core problem with the priesthood in this world, and now it stood in an awkward place. The reason was that people had adopted it as their profession and their chosen path without knowing who they were or what they truly wanted, or what exactly they were getting themselves into. This only led to a revelation somewhere down the line that they had other needs, persuasions or convictions. Sometimes they had matured, grown into an entirely different person. However, by that time, they found themselves too deep into the forest, and as Shakespeare wrote in Macbeth,

'Stepped in so far that, should I wade no more, returning were as tedious as go o'er'.'

It would by then be too late, and these people relented and continued to live lives of quiet desperation against their nature.

Madhav had now had a taste of life outside Holymath. No matter how unusual his set of circumstances, it was a different life and world. Father felt happy about that. Madhav, however, was soon back into the swing of things, and he enjoyed being back. Comfortable in his skin; it was an innate gift as he was able to blossom wherever he was planted.

Meanwhile, in Mumbai, the heat had been turned on as far as Pramod Sinha was concerned. There had been several raids on his various unauthorised joints and criminal hubs, some notably considered too covert for any local law enforcement agency to have instigated them. These threw him as he had no idea who had ordered them, and he was getting increasingly furious.

He used all his clout with the local law enforcement heads, but all he got back was that they had 'orders from somebody at the Centre'. He knew it was not the government, as the ruling political party at the 'Centre' was his. However, he did consider back-stabbing as a possibility because the Opposition leaders did not have the power to instruct such 'raids'. Politics is a dirty game.

As the raids continued, he was getting increasingly agitated and frustrated. He was smart enough and soon concluded that it was some very select, elite, perhaps autonomous authority. He vowed to find out, but in the meantime, some stories about him were beginning to surface on to the public domain via social media. However, the newspapers did not dare put anything in black and white as yet. But they did send their dogs out to sniff around, and would not miss an opportunity for mud-slinging if one arose.

Pramod was not a fool, and he also always considered the possibility of an insider, but who? He did consider Rawat, but he had left more than two years ago; so would be unaware of some of the recent operations which were implicated in these raids. His closest sidekicks, including Ram Singh, were trusted and loyal. He had tested them well; he kept their finances solid, and there was no sign of any suspicious behaviour. They knew he could smell a rat from a mile and he was ruthlessly dangerous and unforgiving, so they dare not defect. Whatever be the case, he was getting increasingly restless, and needed these intrusions to end.

Three days later, there was a significant development, as it often happens when the tide of time turns sour – there can be a cascade of trouble that befalls a person. Such was about to happen to Pramod. Three suspicious terrorists were arrested near Hyderabad; they had been plotting to blow up a famous local monument which is not only the single most recognisable building in Hyderabad but also a nationally loved monument – the Charminar. Through 'chatter' and intelligence that RAW had gathered, they managed to apprehend them two days before the planned attack. Since Krishan was the official head of operations, he decided to be present at some of the interrogation sessions.

Interestingly, when it came to how they had acquired the weapons and RDX required, the trail seemed to end at the doorstep of a local politician in Mumbai. They mentioned him as an arms supplier. Instantly, Krishan considered a possible connection. A few days later, one of the interrogating officers from RAW called Krishan, "Sir, we might be onto something. One of the three terrorists is willing to talk; he broke down, says he does not know any names but might recognize some faces. He says one person was a well-known public figure and that he had accidentally met him, though he was not supposed to. He was certain of this person's involvement in the operation – a prominent political figure in Mumbai."

Krishan said, "Show him pictures of all the local ministers and Members of Parliament in Maharashtra, but don't ask any leading questions as it will not hold up in court." He insisted. "Let's see what he comes up with."

The government of Maharashtra consists of 23 cabinet ministers and 16 ministers of state. Sure enough, after he was shown pictures he pointed unequivocally to the seventeenth photograph shown – the face belonged to Pramod Sinha!

This information led to a meeting within the senior directorate at RAW. The key agenda on the table was to discuss whether any official action could be taken against the man. Keeping well in mind his political prowess and his underworld connections, it was a tough call. Fortunately, the Unlawful Activities (Prevention) Act – UAPA – amended in 2013, was above the intrusion levels and interference by politicians, as it had been created for the highest cause – national security. Even the most deceitful politicians had to bow before it. Krishan felt that they had enough in the testimony of an arrested terrorist, willing to be a witness, to bring Pramod in for questioning.

Early morning long before dawn would break, and the world was still asleep, a 'SWAT-like' team of Special Forces swooped into a fortified Chembur residence of the Member of Parliament, Pramod Sinha. He preferred to live at home rather than at the official ministerial residence provided to him by the state government. The main reason was that he could better control his vast web of illicit operations from there. He had sophisticated computer software, advanced satellite and fibreoptic networks, and a small team of clever, highly paid, dedicated and loyal workers who worked round the clock. There was 24-hour surveillance and tracking of his vast, dark empire. He was wheeling and dealing in stuff to the tune of two hundred million US dollars a year, so it was a pretty substantial and lucrative undertaking!

His residence was quite a fortress. He had two levels of basements from where he controlled his realm. The existence of the second one was known to but a few.

A Special Task Force team had been keeping track of his whereabouts, and they were using UAV's (drones) to maintain their surveillance on him. He had just returned from a whirlwind weekend in Bali. He walked through his front door just past midnight. He was exhausted, had two quick single malts and dropped on to his bed in deep slumber. The squad arrived at about four a.m., stealthily and swiftly surrounded the house and then approached the front door! Initially, his security guards resisted. However, when they were told that there was an unbailable warrant for his arrest and the serious consequences of any resistance, they opened the gates. Pramod was found sleeping in his Hermes pyjamas, naked above the waist. He was furious and uncooperative. He asked to make a call and tried to stall them with blatant threats of, 'Do you know who I am?', but the crack team had none of it. He was by no measure the biggest fish they had roped.

He was detained in an unknown location within a nondescript office building, and not in a prison cell. The idea was to interrogate him since there was no official charge against him as yet. Soon there were high-powered telephone calls, including one from the Prime Minister's office, but fortunately, RAW had autonomy. Krishan's boss had to himself speak to the Prime Minister; Krishan's name never came up.

They planned to make sure that any quick release was not going to take place. Over the following week, while Pramod was still in 'remand', a case was being prepared against him. Not surprisingly, the RAW team ran out of time and luck to find a 'smoking gun' back at his residence. His brilliant information and technology team had cleverly encrypted all the software and all servers related to his activities were remotely located. The Liechtenstein and Luxemburg bank accounts were all cleverly engineered. His various business affairs were based in shell companies in Dubai, Cayman and Jersey islands. All these accounts seemed legitimate and could not be touched by the Government of India, at least not for now. The mafia operations were all in black money, but they could not locate any stashed cash. Extraordinarily and shrewdly, Pramod had kept his official phone records squeaky clean. Later it came to light that he would change his SIM cards daily. He would destroy up to five new SIM cards by the end of each day's business. He was a crafty old dodger, always a step ahead of the game!

With every passing hour, the authorities were put under increasing pressure by an intensifying political crusade to release him. If they could not charge him, they would not be able to hold him for long. Something had to give, and the system did!

On the eighth day, finally, the chief of RAW had to succumb to powers that be and release him. There was no stout evidence to hold him any longer and no ground on which he could be charged. If all they had was a word of a terrorist against that of an eminent politician, it would not hold up in front of a judge. A more robust case would have to be built against him. They would need concrete evidence. Hence, his supposedly non-bailable warrant was quashed by his hot-shot lawyers at the High Courts.

Pramod walked out a free, furious man!

□

21

Although shaken by the recent events, Pramod Sinha was quickly back in the saddle – defiant. He tried not to show that his feathers had been ruffled and for the first time in his long reign, his power questioned. Though thick-skinned, he was secretly perturbed by all the public shaming and exposure as a result of the recent events. His reputation before the ordinary people from his constituency, who were unaware of his dark side, had been severely tarnished. He was aware that it would take a lot to rebuild that bridge. He had considered himself invincible and infallible with the vast web of power that he wielded. He had been riding this wave of over-confidence for so long that he felt a sense of disappointment. Nonetheless, he was a wounded lion, and vowed to strike back hard and swiftly on whosoever was responsible for even considering the notion of trying to take him down.

This mess had put a temporary spanner in his illegal activities. He realised that he might have to tone things down a little, put the brakes on, and also go under the radar for some time. It would be a wise move at least in the short term to work on the innocent and unsuspecting citizens from his constituency and suspend ties with the underworld. The one thing that his infuriated ego was desperate for was to find out who was responsible. He vowed that he would find and destroy that person. His retribution would be ruthless and severe.

He scrutinised his whole staff, starting with his oldest, most trusted employees and confidants. He interrogated and threatened each of them individually. A few heads rolled and he sacked three men from his security team. The next in line was his crooked accountants. They too were taken to task, and thereafter, one by one every domestic and office employee, cook and even janitor were tormented till they were reduced to tears.

He still could not get a definite answer. He realised that this was a high-profile investigation into his affairs and a determined and single-pointed effort to bring him down. Unequivocally, this had to be a personal vendetta. He did have many enemies, but as long as he was in power, he knew none of them would dare to rear their heads against him as they knew the reprisal would be severe.

What was also certain was that there had to be some inside help. But who? That was the million-dollar question that bothered him. It was making him edgy, impatient and very angry. He wanted revenge! As he possessed no moral arc, no compassion and his humanity nothing but a pretence, he was willing to stoop to whatever level and resort to any necessary measure to avenge this humiliation. He was seething inside, and the fire demanded a scalp – now!

He decided to go to Delhi, to see if he could harness information through his resources there. Ironically, the corrupt are often let down by the even more corrupt, especially in politics. The minute something derogatory is in the public domain, they want to quickly distance themselves from the mudslinging. However false and fragile it may be, politicians want their reputation and image to remain untarnished.

Sometimes, to protect the party's interest at large and to seem scrupulously clean, they are happy to incriminate a fellow party member and quite easily disassociate from and sacrifice one of their flock as long as it is in the name of political gain. If necessary, even turn the dogs on them.

Despite his soul seething ire and burning ferocity, Pramod

did not get very far during his visit to the capital. He could immediately sense resistance and even antagonism during his conversations with his comrades. He walked out, disgusted and indignant. He was so preoccupied with his blinding fury that he had let his guard down about what else could be brewing in the volatile political arena and behind his back.

He landed back in Mumbai by the last flight of the day. Much to his surprise, he was met with and discreetly accosted and escorted by some plain-clothes men before he could be received in the lounge by his own. An SUV with dark windows was waiting in the VVIP cordon, and they drove him to a nondescript, unmarked office building. This time around, it was the Central Bureau of Investigations (CBI) who had nabbed him. A new investigation had been initiated against him, in this instance on the premise of money laundering. He was livid that something like this could happen again, in such close succession, and almost had a physical confrontation with them.

The CBI told him they knew about all his nefarious activities, and had enough evidence to indict him. However, due to immense political pressure and the potential backlash of the likes of strikes and political rallies by his party members which would disrupt public life, his enquiry would be held at an internal level, to begin with. If he were found guilty, only then would he be subject to public prosecution.

For the next sixteen days, which felt like a lifetime to Pramod, he had to go through various levels of an inquest. He was permitted to return home by night but under 'house-arrest', he went through high intensity and sustained interrogation during the daytime. He was understandably burning with rage and thinking seriously about fleeing the nest. He had millions stashed in banks abroad, and it would not be too difficult. But then he realised that it could backfire, so decided against it.

Fortunately for him, he was more cunning than a coyote and had covered his tracks rather well. Even though it was evident that he was dirty and guilty as hell, all the enquiry committee members knew that to charge him what was required was stout, irrefutable evidence. Furthermore, it needed to be something apolitical that did not affect the ruling political party as a whole as, in the latter case, it would get quashed by a political sledgehammer. It needed to be an activity in which only he was involved, preferably an issue of national security. Pramod was suspicious that some of his so-called well-wishers in Delhi had set these CBI wheels in motion behind his back while he was there trying to fight his corner.

Unfortunately, they found that yet again there was no illegal activity under which he could be charged. All evidence against him was either incomplete, tainted or inadmissible. On the seventeenth day, they had to throw up their hands again and close the enquiry. He walked away enraged.

This time around, Pramod used this custody as a marketable and political gambit. His cronies, his party members, created a huge furore in the media against RAW, the CBI and the Opposition parties. His supporters and political allies declared it a massive conspiracy. They accused the opposition of these baseless allegations and let the national media know that these enforced enquiries were a political fiasco. Pramod and his party members were finally having a field day! He had a resurgence in his political ratings.

All this, of course, was not enough to appease him. He wanted blood, he wanted a head to hang all of this on. This egomaniacal, narcissistic psychopath was now a deeply wounded animal. One of his security guards raised some doubts about Ram Singh's allegiance. He told Pramod that Ram Singh had been acting a bit strange and cagey lately. Desperate, Pramod had him summoned again, as there were a few things he knew that only a handful of others did. However, Ram Singh was shocked that his loyalty had been questioned. He categorically denied all accusations. Nonetheless, he was physically tortured and beaten to within an inch of his life, but he stuck to his guns and denied any wrongdoing. Pramod's men threatened to take his family to task if they found any evidence, but investigations showed no indication of a money trail or lifestyle change. Neither Ram Singh nor his family had shown any signs of gain. It became increasingly unlikely that he had 'ratted' on his long-term employer.

He was thrown half-alive amongst the gutters near the slums of Mumbra to die from his potentially fatal wounds. Fortunately, the authorities were still watching closely, and Ram Singh was promised safety and protection as per their earlier discussions. He was quickly picked up and taken to a private nursing home and placed under heavy security. All his expenses were taken care of by RAW. He was provided with the best possible medical attention. It took him two months to recover and allowed him plenty of time to lick his wounds. His family hunted for him high and low but came up with nothing; he seemed to have vanished. After more than two months had passed, their hopes of ever finding him alive were dwindling. It seemed like the woeful tale of another small timer that this big, corrupt city had swallowed.

Ram Singh, sadly, understood that he could not chance to get in touch with them. He was better deemed dead. As long as he was considered so, his family was safe. He was like a ship that must stay at sea forever. He ended up with a bit of a limp but otherwise had recovered. He co-operated fully with RAW and provided them all he knew, even the tiniest crumb of information that may be useful.

Once he was deemed fit for discharge, he was transported in the middle of the night in the back of a 3-ton army truck. His relocation was a small group of villages on the periphery of Coimbatore, in southern India. He was established in a small anonymous hamlet and provided a small flat and an adequate stipend to survive on for the rest of his days. In addition, he was given employment at the local post office so that the locals would not question his sudden appearance in their neighbourhood. It was considered a regular transfer within a government post. This was not likely to arouse any suspicions.

He was sternly warned that if he tried to get in touch with his family in a spate of emotion, he would endanger their safety and his.

Over the next few months into his new, lonely existence, he pined for his family but knew that he could not surface. He regularly felt pangs of regret, but convinced himself that he had done the morally correct thing, but was it a price worth paying? It certainly beats being locked up for many years, he told himself time and again. He would have to live amongst the shadows for the rest of his life and his adopted false identity. He was dead to his family and friends alike but still had his life. He grew a thick beard and shaved his head. He also always wore dark glasses and a baseball cap. He did not make any close associations, just kept acquaintances in his new location. 'Such are the wages of sin,' he would time and again whisper under his breath. He now responded to the name Bhanu Pratap.

His disappearance and perhaps death was, however, not enough to appease Pramod, who remained thirsty for blood and continued to look for a definite explanation. Although he had mercilessly got rid of one of his closest aides, he was convinced that Ram Singh alone was incapable of such a coup. Who else could it be? That question hung like a sword of Damocles over his head.

He tried to extend and strengthen his friendship with Arvind. Perhaps there was a sliver of subliminal guilt and on occasion the faintest doubt that he could be behind all this. However, he knew Arvind to be a decent person and did not believe that Arvind either had the fangs or the resources to create a storm on such a grand scale of political manoeuvring and wrangling against him. He got neither a cold shoulder nor any encouragement from Arvind. Madhav's presence had not gone unnoticed. He questioned casually, and all he got back was that Madhav was an orphaned second cousin of his late wife. He swallowed the explanation temporarily, but the particular way the boy stared at him seemed peculiar. He thought there was something wrong with the child.

A few months passed. Madhav had been back and forth to the ashram a couple of times. His mind was still unclear whether he wanted to stay in Mumbai or return to his life as he had always known it to be, back at Holymath. He was still too young to know whether he should take on monkhood or move in permanently with Arvind. Neither Arvind nor Father Edoardo rushed or put any undue pressure on him to decide one way or the other. His education was suffering, although both of them were filling in the blanks as much as possible. Arvind tried to enhance it with some private tuition whenever he was in Mumbai.

What was also happening as a by-product of this was that Arvind was visiting the ashram frequently. This naturally started to rub off on him. He was slowly but steadily imbibing their culture and ways. He was spending more time with Father and other monks. There was one visit when he stayed at Holymath for two whole weeks. He was beginning to benefit from the early morning meditation and found that it had a distinct impact on his thinking. He became calmer, his sleep was no longer so restless, and he also felt less volatile emotionally. He seemed to be able to ease the stranglehold of his past life that had gripped him so intensely.

Meanwhile, nothing much was moving in the Pramod Sinha camp. He was slowly rebuilding his political image, and his evil empire was burgeoning again.

Arvind had all but given up any hope of incriminating him.

□

22

Vagamon became their home for that summer. It was now three months since Arvind and Madhav had been back from Mumbai. The monsoon was now arriving in its boundless glory. The valleys were even greener, and every waterfall resplendent.

A couple of days earlier, they had a most unexpected visitor at Holymath. Father Bernardino all the way from Italy had given everyone a surprise by turning up unannounced at the ashram. Father Edoardo could not believe his eyes!

Father Bernadino was already well aware of the backstory of Madhav and Arvind. He often guided Father Edoardo whenever they spoke over the phone about all that was going on, and what might be the best way forward for Madhav. He was genuinely pleased to meet Madhav and Arvind. Although monk-style, there were celebrations that night, which meant a bit more colour at the dining tables, a few extra candles, a few more dishes, and a couple of expensive bottles of red wine. Still, austere by any other standards.

Madhav and Arvind, both bonded immediately with the benign soul. He had such a warm and benevolent aura that it was hard not to be drawn to him. He spoke to Arvind when Madhav was not present, and expressed his sympathy for Arvind's loss and what he thought about who Madhav was – considering the most unusual way in which his life was unfolding.

On one such visit, Father Edoardo and Arvind decided to sit down with Madhav and have a serious conversation. They tried to explain to the twelve-year-old boy who he might be in terms of his parental lineage. Surreal as it was, he may somehow have imbibed the spirit of the unborn twin, as there was no other explanation for all that he knew and felt, and for his behaviour towards certain people and situations. And, peculiar as it did sound, Arvind was as close to a biological father that he had. It was not easy for any adult, leave alone a child, to accept and comprehend such a concept or possibility. The only redeeming factor here was that Father Edoardo himself was explaining all of this to Madhav. For him, there was no greater authority, as he had been both a father and mother. His word was gospel for Madhav, who also happened to be mature beyond his years.

Analysing his time spent with the boy, Arvind decided that it had been a pleasant experience. To begin with, he could not say that Madhav had evoked any unique paternal feelings; there was just some kinship. But with passing time, he realised a deeper undercurrent, and an inexplicable bond was developing. On a different note and with every passing day, Madhav's schooling became a looming and prime issue, and it bothered Arvind.

In the meantime, Arvind had decided it was time to visit Anamika's parents in Pune to give them a chance to spend some time with Madhav. After all, they had lost not only their daughter but also their grandchild. Arvind and Madhav agreed to make the trip by road. The only issue was that they would pass the same place where the tragic incident had happened. However, considering some water had flowed under the bridge, Arvind felt they would be fine. Also, it would be a test to see if he and Madhav had moved on.

They decided to leave Mumbai early, well before dawn to avoid the heavy traffic of office-goers. It was a wet and drizzly morning. Arvind felt a bit nervous, to begin with, but shrugged off the feeling. Madhav loved the open road, and it was very much as Mehak used to. He sat with his face pressed against the window, and intently absorbed the varied scenery: there was so much diversity with every passing mile. They were quickly on to the Mumbai-Pune expressway and the lap of the Western Ghats. It was an enjoyable drive even on a wet day, and the foliage was a glistening dark green, dense, rich and lustrous. For the entire duration of the journey, Arvind observed him silently, and felt a peculiar feeling overwhelming him.

Arvind thought about taking a DNA test for paternity, but decided against it.

□

23

He was found dead in his small flat located in the outskirts of Coimbatore, still wearing his post office uniform. He had been dead for over four days before his mutilated and rapidly decaying body was discovered. He had been tortured in such a grotesque manner that even the Chinese would get squeamish. Ram Singh's face was disfigured beyond recognition.

It was the lucky break for which Pramod had been waiting. He had stumbled upon a massive piece of the jigsaw in his quest to find out who was shaking his corrupt tree and had managed to tarnish his powerful empire, which he had worked uncompromisingly hard to build. He was evil and ruthless, so power-hungry that he had not let anyone or anything stand in his way. He was inhuman and willing to remove any obstacle; even his own family came second to his colossal web of power. Yet, someone had been able to get to him.

One of his trusted henchmen was visiting some family in Coimbatore and happened to visit the post office where Ram Singh was working as Bhanu Pratap. He was browsing in the post-office-cum-shop when he heard this voice, and it took him just two seconds to know who it was; he knew the voice so well. Still, he could not believe his ears, so he hid behind the shelves and peered at the till. He saw this man who looked quite different, but the demeanour was the same, the eyes too were the same and the voice unmistakable. He was not fooled by the flimsy camouflage of a beard and baseball cap. He was confident it was Ram Singh. He quietly slipped out of the building and phoned his boss in Mumbai.

Ram Singh provided every morsel of information before his last agonising breath.

It was the best piece of news Pramod had received in the last few months – devil's luck! Arvind? He could not believe it! How could this benign, impotent, depressed, pathetic doctor, whom he had virtually destroyed and whose soul he had practically crushed, have the guile to raise his head against the mighty Sinha empire! This little ant had given him no end of grief in the last few months. He decided that Arvind would pay for it gravely. He had to get Arvind and swore that he would subject him to such a torturous death that Ram Singh's spirit would feel let off lightly.

He quickly found out more details from Arvind's unsuspecting parents about him and Munnar. He immediately dispatched two of his best and most skilful 'dogs' by the first available flight to Kochi. They were in Munnar within seven hours of leaving Mumbai. They headed straight for the cottage but did not find anybody there. They broke into the cottage and ravaged it, turning it inside out, but there was no clue to Arvind's present whereabouts. They next went into the annexe. There was enough evidence to see that Arvind was the one who lived there, but again no trail as to where he was.

Since Arvind and Demitri stayed pretty much to themselves, there was nobody to ask. They tried to find out who was their domestic help by questioning a few tea estate workers. It still took them two full days to locate the maid who came every morning to cook and clean for Demitri and occasionally for Arvind. She was unsure but did mention the town of Vagamon and also the word ashram. It was enough for them to go by, and on the third day, they left for Vagamon, searching for their mark.

At the same time as the thugs found out where Arvind was and left for Vagamon, the telephone in the foyer of the Holymath

Ashram rang off the hook. Eventually, one of the monks picked it up, and the person at the end of the line wanted to speak to Dr Arvind, stating that it was an emergency. Arvind was quite surprised to receive a phone call. He was immediately anxious, and his first thought was whether something had happened to his parents. He spoke anxiously into the mouthpiece, "This is Arvind here."

The voice at the other end spoke in a hushed tone, "Sir, this is Rawat speaking."

"Rawat!" exclaimed a surprised Arvind.

"Yes, sir. I am sorry to call you, but I need to give you some important information. As you know, I have been tracking the activities in the Sinha camp as I still have a few friends there. It seems that they have found Ram Singh and have settled the score with him, and two days ago, two of Pramod Sinha's most dangerous men have left for Kochi. They are looking for you. I think you could be in serious trouble, sir."

Of course, he was not privy to the details about Arvind's involvement or responsibility for all the shake-up of Pramod's businesses.

"I think your life is in danger, sir," he said. Being forthright, he was still attempting to atone for his sins.

Arvind was in a bit of a shock as he put the phone down. He was thankful for Rawat's vigilance. 'What now?' he thought. He had to act swiftly and decisively and had seen and known enough about Pramod and his brutal ways to realise that time was of the essence. He immediately went over to speak to Father Edoardo and Father Bernardino, who were well aware of the chain of events and the seriousness of the matter at hand. The three of them sat silent for some time and pondered over what to do next.

Then Father Bernardino spoke, slowly and deliberately, "One thing is clear, that we need to get you and Madhav to safety, and well beyond the reach of this man and his cronies. He is immensely powerful and resourceful, and I am not sure where you could hide from him in this country."

"Have you got your passports?" Fortuitously, he and Madhav had had their passports made while they were living in Mumbai. It was Krishan who had suggested that they do so.

"I think we need to get you out of this country."

"What! How?" questioned Arvind.

Father Bernardino had thought this through before he had started speaking, "There is an Italian Consulate located in Chennai; ordinarily, a letter from me would be enough to get you an Italian visa. I know the ambassador personally. In this instance, I will accompany you to avoid hiccups, get you a visa, and put you on a flight to Italy and safety before anyone can get to you. I will call the monastery in Sicily, and your stay will be arranged. We have no time to lose; we should leave straight away!"

Within half an hour, all four of them, with Demitri the driver at the helm as he insisted that they shouldn't travel by taxi, were on their way to Kochi. They had booked a flight from there to Chennai, and the following morning from Chennai to Naples on Alitalia.

Midway to Kochi, at the resplendent Marmala waterfall, the yellow Beetle crossed a taxi. It was carrying Pramod's henchmen headed in the opposite direction.

They did not even glance at the Beetle.

□

24

Hours after they left for Naples, two muscled men arrived at Holymath Ashram. They visited under the pretext of wanting to look around. Everyone at the ashram had already been made aware, and they were greeted and treated like any other visitor, shown around and given unrestricted access. Nobody said anything, and there was nothing to hide. The birds had flown the nest. They would have to return to Mumbai empty-handed with their tails tucked between their legs. They were pretty terrified, knowing their boss would not be pleased.

Alitalia flight A 372 landed at Capodichino airport in Naples on time in the early hours of the morning. When Arvind and Madhav came out of the airport, they were received by monks from Father Bernardino's diocese in Sicily. It was easy to spot them as their robes were a giveaway. They drove to the southern tip of the country and then took a boat across the Strait of Messina. It was a gentle two-mile ferry crossing into Sicily.

Three days later, Father Bernardino also flew in to join them. He let them know that men from Mumbai had come looking for them and that Arvind and Madhav had escaped in the nick of time. The visitors were cared for as special guests of Father Bernardino. Soon, a week passed, and they had settled in nicely. Daily, visitors came to seek counsel from Father as he was highly respected in the region by people of all faiths. On one such occasion, Father mentioned that he wanted Arvind to meet a particular person.

Antonio Gufoni was born with an angelic disposition, yet his surname invoked terror because he was one of the sons of Salvatore Gufoni, who was now 88-years old. Salvatore was the head of an infamous and imperious mafia family. They had ruled over the underworld of Sicily for the last fifty years. Antonio was the youngest of the three sons, and somewhat estranged from the family. Fazio and Gino, his two older brothers, were still very much into the family business and more feared than respected across Sicily.

Antonio was undoubtedly a misfit in his own home. Ever since he was a young boy, he was different from his brothers, and he had a kind and benevolent nature – gentle as can be, loving and forgiving. He was also blessed with an acutely perceptive nature. From a tender age, he became aware of the nature of his family business. He had never showed the slightest inclination towards it, nor did he possess any qualities required to make a successful underworld kingpin. He was an intellectual, reserved and introspective child. His interests lay elsewhere: in world history, literature, the animal kingdom and theology. However, his father would have none of it and was convinced that he had the ruthless Gufoni gene, and that it was only a matter of time before his wayward son would blossom and become like his older brothers, who had taken to the family business like fish to water. 'You don't need to teach a canary to sing, do you?'

To add to this, as he turned eighteen, Antonio fell in love with sixteen-year-old Maria. She was an innocent and beautiful young lady who also happened to be the goddaughter of Father Bernardino. Antonio had first seen her during a church service. After that, he never missed a single one. He knew that she would never tie the knot with him, given the nature of his family business. Peculiar as it seems, the Gufoni family had good relations with Father Bernardino and held him in the highest regard. In fact, from time to time, they would come to seek his counsel.

Father Bernardino was a true man of faith, and though he was aware of the nature of their work, he believed that it was not for him to judge them. He was there to show them the right path if they were willing.

When Antonio eventually revealed that he had decided never to join the family business and wished to marry Maria, Salvatore was livid! His Italian blood boiled, and he chose to disown and exile his youngest son, following an impassioned and emotional fit of temper. Antonio had expected that exact reaction and was prepared to forego whatever was necessary for his love. He was all set to leave home.

Before he could walk out, his two older brothers Fazio and Gino, intervened. They were more than ten years older than him; both doted on their younger brother and were very protective of him. They convinced their father that there was no reason to induct Antonio into the business forcibly and that he was not built for it. Besides, they could manage the business perfectly well between the two of them. Salvatore grudgingly, and after much raving and ranting, relented, and accepted the situation. Antonio did not waste a second approaching Father for his God-daughter's hand in marriage. Since he had himself christened Antonio, and seen this boy grow up in front of his eyes, he was well aware of the character and qualities of this young man and had no hesitation that his God-daughter would be in good hands. He blessed the couple.

Father Bernardino introduced Madhav and Arvind to his son-in-law. They all shook hands warmly and sat after their evening meal for coffee. Antonio and Maria now had a beautiful daughter called Anabella. Father explained the circumstances under which the two had come to Sicily.

It was then Antonio said, "Arvind, Maria and I were also expecting twins, and everything was going smoothly but sadly, one twin who was a boy was stillborn at term. It was a tough period for us, so I can completely understand what you and your wife must have gone through."

Arvind felt an immediate kinship with him. When they discussed the minutiae of the events that had led them to flee their country, Pramod Sinha's name came up.

"That name sounds strangely familiar," said Antonio, "but I cannot be certain." He wondered if one of his brothers might have mentioned it or whether it was because he was a high-profile politician from India. Possibly his name might have been mentioned on the news or brought up at the family dinner table. Although he lived a simple and honest life, quite unlike the rest of his family, he remained very close to both his brothers.

"Let me ask my brothers, as they are into various projects worldwide, including India, and I wonder if they are aware of this person."

With that, they shook hands and decided to catch up very soon.

Arvind did not expect the meeting to have any meaningful outcome.

□

25

Back in Mumbai, the temperature was high. The goons had returned empty-handed and without the faintest clue about the whereabouts of Arvind and Madhav, as though they had disappeared into thin air! Pramod had contacts and resources everywhere. He ordered his staff to scan all railway stations and national airline reservations about where they might have gone. All major bus terminals were being monitored. However, even he could never envision that they could have escaped overseas, and he did not consider looking into international airline travel. Sicily, of course, would not even have occurred in his wildest imaginings.

Meanwhile, Antonio had conferred with his brothers, and he was genuinely surprised to learn that they had had some dealings with Pramod Sinha in the recent past. When he explained the predicament of Arvind and Madhav, his brothers wanted to meet them.

Arvind met Fazio and Gino Gufoni. The meeting was at one of their vast hilltop Sicilian mansions overlooking the beautiful Mediterranean. Both the brothers were impeccably dressed in Rubinacci pin-stripe, three-piece suits. They sat out in the immaculately manicured gardens, with a soft breeze blowing northwards from the sea. The massive Carrara marble veranda was surrounded by beautiful eighteenth-century Italian sculptures. In front was an expansive portico with gilded arches. It was just after twilight and the setting was a sight to behold, though, at that point, Arvind was oblivious to its beauty. They were warm, gracious and polite towards him.

It came to light that Pramod had dealings with them in the past for illegal arms and *hawala* transactions. Occasionally, he was also involved in small shipments of cocaine. Over the last three years, they had executed substantial transactions. About six months ago, Pramod had directly approached Fazio, asking him for a favour. He had a friend who had business interests in Italy and owned a large construction company. His name was Rishi Bhatt. He was rooting for a huge contract: the construction of a vast shopping mall to be built on the outskirts of Palermo. The Gufonis could swing it his way if they wanted, and so they did, for a handsome purse.

Unfortunately, Rishi was a bad apple; he had planned to siphon off as much money as possible and had no intentions of doing a proper job on the mall. It was evident from the first week the construction started that the project was always going to be a non-starter. He swallowed a substantial initial payment from the Sicilian government, fled Sicily and was untraceable. Though their pockets had been lined by the Gufonis, the authorities still expected a good job to be done. They came back to the Gufonis, bitterly disappointed. This was a big blow to the Gufonis' reputation as, though they were corrupt, they were still good for their word and had always delivered the goods. This time the authorities were displeased with the Gufonis. Fortunately, the family had deep pockets and had to spend a lot of their own money to put the project back on track. They contacted Pramod, who apologised but said that he was unaware of Rishi's misdemeanour, and there was not much he could do as he had no idea where Rishi had disappeared to. The brothers were unhappy with his explanation and felt he had to take some responsibility as the deal was made through, and because of, him. The whole matter left a big chip on the Gufoni shoulders.

Having heard Arvind's full story, the brothers were even

more enraged about how Pramod had destroyed Arvind's family and life in a premeditated way. As it is, they were naturally sympathetic given Father Bernardo's involvement, and became even more so. They promised to help if they could. There was already enough annoyance and indignation; it did not need more impetus. They were also surprised by, and unaware of the extent and ramifications of Pramod's international operations. It was already agreed that the family would have no dealings with him in future. Gufonis always tried to avoid corrupt politicians outside Italy. Sometimes, however, dealing with them was unavoidable.

Being the mafia, they were, of course, masters of retribution and teaching people lessons. Once they find that they have been rubbed the wrong way, God save the offenders! They gave the matter their time, attention and serious thought. They had their people tracking clandestine chatter on the various platforms and markets relating to illegal arms, narcotics and human trafficking over the next two weeks. They were sure that his name would eventually pop up somewhere in these Chinese whispers. Sure enough, it did, and sooner than they thought.

A large shipment of Kalashnikovs and AK67 assault rifles was being moved from Morocco, via Italy and then across Afghanistan for a militant group in the northwest peninsula. Guess who the arms dealer was – though very much from the shadows. The contraband was split into staggered shipments and through various modes and routes. Part of it was being carried by Pramod personally as he was visiting Sicily at that time. He had diplomatic immunity through airport customs due to his ministerial status, so smuggling was easy. Moreover, he had all the Indian customs officials on his tab. The Gufoni brothers paid a king's ransom for the arms' drop-off and pick-up information.

The mafia knows how to use their connections timely. More often than not, it is to line their coffers or as a 'get-out-of-jail' card. But this time, it was for an entirely different matter.

It was a tip-off to the Italian Special Operation Department (R.O.S. Caltanissetta) of the Carabinieri Arma dei Carabinieri, provided this time by the Cosa Nostra themselves. They planned the sting operation meticulously and swooped swiftly and decisively on the small fishing trawler as it eased into a little-used and tucked away harbour of Sicily near Siracusa. It was just past three in the morning. They quickly made a pact with the accosted offenders, who were stunned by the sheer number of police officers that had descended on them. Freedom in exchange for information about who was involved was promised. This led to the confirmation of the involvement of Pramod Sinha. Within thirty minutes, two hundred and fifty kilometres away, another crack team was at the door of the Presidential Suite of the Rocco Forte Villa Hotel in Palermo. They did not knock but stealthily slipped into the suite with the management's master key. Pramod Sinha was found stark naked in his bed with two Sicilian beauties, one on either side.

He was caught unawares. By the time he got to protesting, showing his indignation and flexing his ministerial and diplomatic muscles, he was unceremoniously handcuffed and on his way to a particular Italian prison cell.

The Indian Prime Minister and his cabinet woke up to the news of his arrest. It was splashed worldwide by Reuters, the international news and global media conglomerate, who for some reason, gave it a lot of attention. Information had been passed personally to the press as a hand-out by Fazio.

There was a high-level parliamentary committee meeting held in New Delhi the same afternoon. The Prime Minister's office was grappling with what to say to the press and the media. They knew that they must distance the ruling party from the Pramod Sinha scandal to avoid a massive political and public backlash. They suspended him *in absentia* from their party and relieved him of his cabinet post. Their press secretary told the waiting press that they were already enquiring into his affairs and the process had been underway for the last few months, and they had suspected him of being involved in illegal activities. The information had been kept under wraps and away from the public domain for obvious reasons. His closest allies and so-called friends also realised that it was a 'poisoned chalice' to stand by Pramod at this point in the wake of this massive scandal that was surely going to finish him. They, too, hastily changed their stance.

Mr. Sinha's house of cards was collapsing quickly.

□

26

Both sets of parents were waiting restlessly outside the arrival lounge at Mumbai airport when the flight from Milan landed – overjoyed at the safe return home of Arvind and Madhav. They were well aware of all that had elapsed and knew a lot more than the press, the local police or politicians. Demitri had flown in from Kochi to join the welcoming committee.

It was common knowledge that Pramod Sinha was now incarcerated in an Italian prison, fighting for extradition to India. The Italian government had firmly refused the request, knowing fully well that he might well escape the stick of the law back home. Moreover, he had upset Italian sentiment, and they were infuriated.

The political establishment in India, too, did not want him back for obvious reasons. They knew if he were outside the country, the press would quickly lose interest, and all furore would soon fade away, and it would be yesterday's news.

While they were in Italy, Father Bernadino had given them some wise counsel, and after conferring with Father Edoardo, it was agreed that Arvind and Madhav would settle down in Lonavala. Mumbai held too many harsh reminders of the past for Arvind. Anamika seemed alive at every street corner, in every café. Arvind would start a new medical practice, and Madhav would attend the local school there. An unusual choice though, as it was so close to where they had lost Mehak and Anamika. They would still be in relative proximity of the parents from both sides. Over the next few days, they packed up their things. Once all arrangements were made, they drove from Mumbai to Lonavala. Demitri went along to help them settle in. He would leave back for Munnar in ten days. He had decided to sell his cottage, and join the brotherhood at Holymath!

They decided for one last time to stop at the site of the accident. This time around, they were both calm though solemn, as though they had got closure.

Madhav laid some flowers by the side of the road, stood with his hands folded and head bowed, and whispered a prayer. They both stepped back from the edge of the road, as the sun set behind the Western Ghats.

Madhav looked up at Arvind, took his hand and softly said, "Shall we go, Dad?"

□□□